The Legends of Mansfield Town

The Legends of Mansfield Town

Dave Bracegirdle and Steve Hartshorn

breedon **books**

PUBLISHING

First published in Great Britain in 2004 by
The Breedon Books Publishing Company Limited
Breedon House, 3 The Parker Centre, Derby, DE21 4SZ.

ISBN 1 85983 435 3

Printed and bound by Cromwell Press, Trowbridge, Wiltshire

Contents

Acknowledgements

YOU CAN always find something to talk about in the hour before kick-off and this book is the product of one such discussion, held at Field Mill before an FA Cup tie against Burnley in January 2004.

Needless to say, many other people became involved along the way. Our grateful thanks must go to Steve Caron and Susan Last at Breedon Books for their faith and expertise.

When our memories failed or we couldn't corroborate our facts, we knew where to turn to for help. For many years Martin Shaw and Paul Taylor have gathered every available scrap of information on Mansfield Town and their help was invaluable.

The Chad has brought news of the club's exploits to generations of followers and their assistance with this publication has been greatly appreciated. John Lomas, the Sports Editor, and Roger Grayson, Chief Photographer, graciously approved the use of many of the photographs included. Our sincere thanks go to them.

Dan Westwell and Chris Bradshaw also provided us with several of their own photographs, for which, again, we are extremely grateful.

Peter Wynne Thomas kindly supplied us with the photograph of Cyril Poole.

Our thanks go to Rob Ferguson, the club's Press Officer, the staff at Mansfield 103.2, and all connected with the *Follow The Yellow Brick Road* fanzine for helping with the advertising.

Research for this book has brought us into contact with many managers, players and officials from Mansfield Town, both past and present, and we hope we've accurately recreated some of their Field Mill memories.

Finally, a big thank you to our partners, Karen and Emma, who've shown admirable patience over the six months it took to turn our chat into *The Legends of Mansfield Town*.

We hope you enjoy it!

Dave Bracegirdle and Steve Hartshorn, July 2004

Foreword

SINCE becoming Chairman in 1993, I've become increasingly aware of the important role the Football Club plays in our local community.

Reading this book illustrates to me how much that has always been the case. Generations of Stags supporters have flocked to Field Mill in hope and expectancy.

Occasionally their dreams have been fulfilled – great matches have been witnessed and heroes have emerged. In truth, on the field success has been sporadic down the years but when it does appear it has been enjoyed by far more than just the loyal few.

I will always treasure the memories of last May, even though the result didn't go in our favour. To see so many Mansfield Town supporters making the journey down to the Millennium Stadium was heart-warming. The flags and banners on display illustrated just how much the club means to so many people.

To be Chairman of the club on such an important occasion as a play-off final was a very proud moment for me personally and to share it with around 14,000 of our supporters confirms my belief that the club is making the right strides forward.

The Legends of Mansfield Town recalls some of the great personalities and characters that have been associated with our fine club. It has been researched and written for the benefit of everyone who has ever taken an interest in our story – I hope you will enjoy it!

Keith Haslam
Chairman, Mansfield Town FC

Rod Arnold

Date of birth: 3 June 1952, Wolverhampton

Mansfield Town record:

Appearances: League 440, FA Cup 24, League Cup 29
Debut: 6 February 1971 v Fulham (a) drew 0–0

Also played for: Wolves

NO ONE has played more games for Mansfield Town than Rod Arnold, a record that the former goalkeeper is proud to hold.

'Personal achievements don't come along all that often in football', he says. 'It's the icing on the cake to have one that may never be broken.'

Rod's final tally of 440 league appearances might even have been higher, had Wolves accepted an offer for his services a year earlier.

'I spent a loan spell at Mansfield and the club were keen to sign me on a permanent basis. Wolves had qualified for the UEFA Cup and manager Bill McGarry wanted me to stay for one more season at Molineux as cover for Phil Parkes.'

Wolves went all the way to the UEFA Cup final, losing to Spurs in an all-English showdown but, as a non-playing sub, Rod didn't even get a medal for his season of inactivity.

After another short loan spell at Field Mill, Rod eventually became a full-time Stag in the summer of 1973 and played his part as the reliable back line of defence for the two Championship successes of the 1970s.

'We had a decent side – a good set of lads – and there were many happy memories. I'll never forget the reception at Field Mill as we did a lap of honour after collecting the Division Four title.'

His memory of the second title is a little cloudier. 'In our final match at Wrexham I was wiped out just before half-time. Their centre-forward Billy Ashcroft took me, the ball, everything. I didn't know where I was. I was feeling groggy and I suppose I must have been concussed but I didn't remember half-time or anything else afterwards until 25 to five. I know that was the time because I recall suddenly having full vision again and being able to see a clock on a church tower outside the Racecourse Ground. We won the game but the celebrations were a little surreal for me as I hadn't remembered much of it!'

Bravery typified Rod's performances in the Mansfield goal. His appearance record bears testament to his fitness and his determination to play but he did have to miss out after breaking an arm.

'It was against Bournemouth at home. I connected with the ball and the back of Adie Burrows's head at the same time. Jeff Lee, the physio, came on and strapped it up and I played on for the last 20 minutes as we hadn't got a substitute goalie. They found out that my ulna was broken and I missed the last nine games of that season.'

Rod still has a framed copy of the *Chad*, celebrating his 400th league appearance for the club, made against Hartlepool in November 1983.

After an association of almost 14 years with the Stags, Rod put his goalkeeping experiences to good use by turning to the coaching side of the game. At the end of the 2003–04 season he celebrated his ninth season as part of Hull City's backroom staff.

Terry Austin

Date of birth: 1 February 1954, Isleworth, Middlesex

Mansfield Town record:

Appearances: League 84, FA Cup 3, League Cup 9
Goals: League 31, FA Cup 1, League Cup 3
Debut: 31 March 1979 v Chester (a) drew 1–1

Also played for: Crystal Palace, Ipswich Town, Plymouth Argyle, Walsall, Huddersfield Town,
Doncaster Rovers, Northampton Town, Stamford Town

TERRY Austin was a Stag for little more than 18 months, yet no one could question his reliability during his time at Field Mill.

During his spell with the club, Mansfield Town's first team played a total of 96 league and cup games – and Terry played in every one!

Lean and mean, Terry really did serve himself up as a goal-scoring machine at Walsall before attracting interest from the Stags. A deal was arranged, with Dave Syrett going the other way to join the Saddlers. Austin's first game for the Yellows was away at Chester, marking the occasion with a debut goal.

Terry's impressive start to life with Mansfield continued, with a goal at Hillsborough that helped his side to an impressive win over Sheffield Wednesday.

By the end of the 1978–79 season things had gone well for the striker but his club endured a summer of turmoil, with the departure of manager Billy Bingham and the arrival of Mick Jones, his replacement. A miserable season followed and the Stags were relegated at the end of it, but Terry's credentials had remained unscathed. He had hit 19 goals in the league, including a hat-trick in the 5–1 home win over Rotherham United, a rare success for the side.

Back in Division Four, Austin began the new season with a bang, scoring both goals in an opening day victory at Halifax Town. Before the match it was revealed that Terry had submitted a written transfer request, hoping to continue his career at a higher level.

Despite his intentions to move, no one could fault Terry's desire or commitment. In early November he netted his second hat-trick for the club, away at Rochdale, turning in a performance which was sure to have raised a few eyebrows. Sure enough, a significant bid for his services was received and Terry moved to Huddersfield Town for a £100,000 fee. The Terriers, at that time, were managed by Ian Greaves, later to take charge at Field Mill.

Austin netted 10 goals in 39 appearances for Huddersfield before continuing his career at Doncaster Rovers and then Northampton Town. He top-scored for the Cobblers in 1983–84, his final season in league football, before being lured into the non-league game with Stamford Town.

After finally hanging up his boots Terry remained in the Mansfield area, working as an executive for an insurance company.

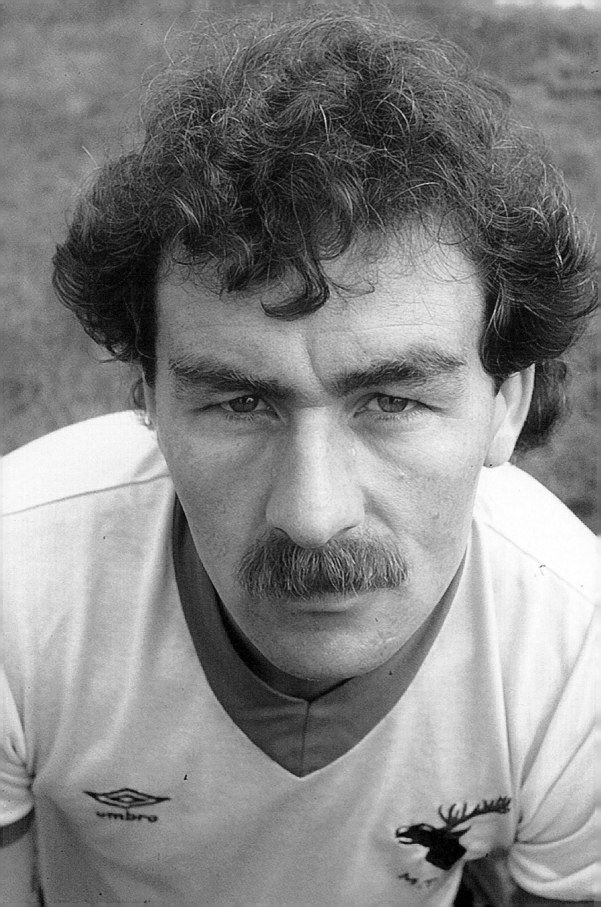

Billy Ayre

Date of birth:	7 May 1952, Crookhill, Co. Durham
Died:	16 April 2002

Mansfield Town record:

Appearances:	League 67, FA Cup 3, League Cup 2, Others 4
Goals:	League 7, FA Cup 0, League Cup 0, Others 0
Caretaker manager:	2 matches (Jan/Feb 1983)
Debut:	28 August 1982 v Blackpool (h) won 2–1

Also played for:	Scarborough, Hartlepool United, Halifax Town
Managed:	Halifax Town, Blackpool, Scarborough, Cardiff City

ALBEIT for the briefest of spells, Billy Ayre can claim to be among the few who have both played and managed the Stags.

He was aged 30 when he signed for Mansfield Town in the summer of 1982. A solid defender, of the stopper variety, he was brought in by boss Stuart Boam from Halifax Town, where he had been both captain and player-coach.

He scored on his first appearance in a Stags jersey in a pre-season match in the Football League Trophy, against Northampton Town, at Field Mill.

The side struggled in the first half of that season and inevitably the manager paid the price for a series of poor results. A new appointment had to be made but, as an interim measure, Billy was given the job of caretaker manager until the arrival of Ian Greaves.

Greaves had connections and persuaded Manchester United to bring a team to Field Mill for a friendly soon after his arrival. Billy, now back in just a playing role, played a starring role in the Stags line-up that brought off an impressive 3–0 victory against the likes of Macari, McGrath, Buchan, Wilkins, Hughes, Gidman and Grimes.

As a player with Scarborough, Billy Ayre twice won the FA Trophy before entering the professional game. He then made over 300 Football League appearances, 67 of them for the Stags, spread over two seasons. Always dangerous at set pieces, he enjoyed the rare luxury of netting twice in a 3–4 home defeat to Wrexham in March 1984.

At the end of that season he was released, returning to his former club Halifax Town. It was with the Shaymen that Billy took on his first full-time managerial appointment. He spent four years in charge there before moving to Blackpool in 1990.

He won a Manager of the Month Award with the Seasiders and helped them to promotion, via the play-offs, in the 1991–92 season. Billy's spell at Bloomfield Road coincided with the club establishing a run of 24 unbeaten home matches, stretching over 12 calendar months! Less successful managerial appointments at both Scarborough and Cardiff City then followed.

Billy was working as a coach with Bury when it was reported that he was battling against lymph node cancer. He died in 2002, peacefully in his sleep with his family around him, aged just 49.

Andy Preece, manager of Bury at the time, said 'Billy was such an easy fellow to get on with and he could always make you laugh at any time. His knowledge of the game was second to none. He was the ultimate professional.'

Eddie Barks

Date of birth: 1 September 1921, Ilkeston, Derbyshire

Mansfield Town record:

Appearances: League 213, FA Cup 12
Goals: League 6, FA Cup 1
Debut: 29 January 1949 v Darlington (h) drew 2–2

Also played for: Heanor Town, Nottingham Forest

ONE OF the most loveable characters to play for the club was Edwin Barks. He was a hard-working, old-fashioned wing-half, who served the Stags well over a seven-season stretch.

As a youngster he had first come to prominence playing non-league football for Heanor Town. The Nottingham Forest scouts were made aware of his potential and he was the first signing made by new manager Billy Walker after his appointment in March 1939.

Barks had to wait several seasons before establishing himself in the first team and only played a total of 66 times for the Reds during his 10-year association with the club. Desperate for first-team football, Eddie made the short trip to Field Mill in January 1949, signing for the sum of £1,000. His Mansfield Town career began in a positive vein, with a goal on his debut against Darlington.

Roy Goodall had been in charge of the club at the time of Eddie's arrival but he soon made way for player/manager Freddie Steele. Gates were healthy and the club's fortunes were on the up. During the 1950–51 season Town advanced to the Fifth Round of the FA Cup.

The prize was a trip to Bloomfield Road to take on Blackpool, arguably the best side in the country at the time. Hopes were high of an upset in front of a crowd of 33,060 but, tactically, the Stags got it wrong. Eddie was employed as a man-marker on Stanley Matthews, Blackpool's most likely match-winner. Barks didn't give the England winger a kick throughout the 90 minutes but his own creativity was missed and the tie was lost. Consolation, however, came in the league, as the Stags finished in second spot in the table.

Frequently prone to injury, Eddie's most consistent season came in 1951–52, when he played in all but one of the games. Cheerful by nature, he would usually have the broadest of grins, no matter what the situation.

He had a loathing of training. His week could never go quickly enough so he could concentrate on match-days when the serious business of competition would begin. Capable of playing in many positions, his versatility often counted against him. Playing under four different managers at Town he would frequently be moved out wide or in the middle of the park and even had a spell as a central defender.

Throughout his time with the club, Eddie was always held in the highest of esteem. On 28 April 1954 Notts County brought a side to Field Mill to play a testimonial game for him and teammate Sid Watson. As a tribute to both players, Stanley Matthews turned up to 'guest' for Mansfield Town.

Before retiring, Eddie played on for one more season, with his final game for the club coming in March 1955, away at Chester.

Joe Beresford

Date of birth: 26 February 1906, Chesterfield
Died: March 1978, Birmingham

Mansfield Town record:

Appearances: League 24, FA Cup 3, Others 8
Goals: League 12, FA Cup 1, Others 5
Debut: 28 August 1926 v Rotherham United Reserves (h) drew 1–1

Also played for: Mexborough, Aston Villa, Preston North End, Swansea Town, Stourbridge, Hartlepools United

THERE haven't been too many Mansfield Town players who've gone on to represent England and play in an FA Cup final. Throw in a Welsh Cup final appearance, and a couple of Division One runners-up medals, and you'll appreciate that Joe Beresford made his mark in the game.

Chesterfield-born, Joe was a superb passer of the ball and represented the Stags in the period just before they joined the Football League. He'd made his mark at Mexborough – smashing in a phenomenal 60 goals in just two seasons. A small fee exchanged hands as Joe moved to Mansfield ahead of the 1926–27 season.

An ever-present – Stags only played 24 league matches – he helped the side to a runners-up slot in the Midland Combination. The club played in lots of local tournaments at that time, and won the Mansfield Hospital Charity Cup, the Notts Benevolent Bowl and the Notts FA Senior Cup during a record-breaking season. In the County Cup semi-final Joe scored his only Stags' hat-trick, although it wasn't particularly decisive: Town beat Sutton Junction 15–1!

During the season, the Stags player/manager Teddy Davison had rebuffed several enquiries from clubs interested in signing Joe. On the last day of the season, however, came an offer the club could not refuse.

Away at Stockport, Joe Beresford was inspirational. Playing at inside-left he carved open the home defence time after time with astute distribution and sensational dribbling skills. Legend has it that an Aston Villa scout was present, intending to run the rule over the Stockport goalkeeper. Beresford's performance turned his eye to such an extent that a bid of £750 was immediately tabled. Mansfield had to accept that sort of money and Joe became a Villan after just one season as a Stag.

Joe walked straight into the Aston Villa first team and was an integral part of the side that twice became league runners-up. He gained selection for a Football League representative XI and appeared for England against Czechoslovakia in 1934.

After eight successful years at Villa Park Joe signed for Preston North End, and appeared in their losing 1937 FA Cup Final side. He later played for Swansea Town, winning a Welsh Cup final medal, before joining Stourbridge. Joe retired from football in 1941, although he came out of retirement to make one appearance for Hartlepools United during an emergency in 1943.

Billy Bingham

Date of birth: 5 August 1931, Belfast

Mansfield Town record:

Manager: March 1978 to July 1979

Played for: Glentoran, Sunderland, Luton Town, Everton, Port Vale, Northern Ireland
(56 caps)

Also managed: Southport, Plymouth Argyle, Linfield, Greece, Everton, PAOK Salonika,
Northern Ireland

MANY Stags supporters have wondered how things would have turned out, had Billy Bingham remained at Field Mill. Seven months after leaving the club he had been installed, for the second time, as the Northern Ireland national team manager, leading them to qualification for successive World Cup Finals.

As a player, Billy had tasted the high life. He had won 56 caps for his country, and enjoyed lengthy and productive stints at both Sunderland and Everton, as well as appearing in the 1959 FA Cup final for Luton Town, against Nottingham Forest.

A broken leg, sustained while playing for Port Vale in 1964, meant a premature retirement as a player. His tactical nouse and love of the game ensured a swift transition to the coaching ranks, initially at Southport. Elevation to the manager's berth brought instant rewards, with the Division Four runners-up slot, and promotion, in 1967.

Billy then managed Plymouth Argyle before his first stint as the national coach for Northern Ireland. Spells with Linfield, the Greek national team, Everton and PAOK Salonika preceded his appointment as manager of Mansfield Town.

The Stags were floundering in the lower reaches of Division Two, in their only season at that level, when Billy was appointed. A debut success against Hull City brought hope of unlikely salvation but the writing had been on the wall for some time and relegation followed.

A decent run in the Anglo-Scottish Cup competition, before semi-final defeat to Burnley, was the highlight of the next, indifferent, season. Relegation for the second successive term was avoided but greater things had been expected of Bingham's side.

During the subsequent close-season Luton Town expressed an interest in signing one of Mansfield's star performers, local youngster Mick Saxby. It is reported that preliminary negotiations took place while Billy Bingham was holidaying in Australia. Upon his return the talks progressed, with Luton striker Steve Taylor becoming part of the proposed deal.

Before the deal was completed, Billy changed his mind. The Mansfield board insisted that the transfer went ahead. When the manager refused to sanction it, he was dismissed from his post. It was an unsavoury end to a relatively unsuccessful stint in charge of the Yellows, but Billy Bingham was soon back in football and, very soon, became a household name.

His Northern Ireland side produced one of the greatest international results of all time, beating hosts Spain during the 1982 World Championships. Billy didn't forget his former club, either. Mansfield Town defender John McClelland won the first six of his 53 caps while still at Field Mill.

Billy's 14-year stint as Northern Ireland manager ended in 1994, at the age of 63. He later joined the board of Blackpool.

Kevin Bird

Date of birth: 7 August 1952, Armthorpe, Doncaster

Mansfield Town record:

Appearances: League 377, FA Cup 24, League Cup 31, Others 18
Goals: League 55, FA Cup 1, League Cup 6, Others 1
Debut: 21 October 1972 v Chester (h) won 4–1

Also played for: Doncaster Rovers, Huddersfield Town

WITH Kevin Bird it was always a case of 'What you see is what you get'. He had passion and commitment in abundance and was a real 'heart on your sleeve' type of footballer. A terrific servant to Mansfield Town, the big defender figures high on the list of the club's leading appearance–makers, spending 11 seasons fighting for the cause.

That the Stags should have benefited from such an outstanding clubman was down to a miscalculation by Doncaster Rovers, Kevin's home-town team. They let him go, early in his career, because they were not fully convinced about his potential. One man who was sure enough was Frank Marshall. He had been a coach at Rovers and had moved to Field Mill as assistant to Danny Williams. The young defender was given a three-month trial and never looked back.

'They were great times', recalls Kevin. 'Everyone seemed to get on really well with each other, which was important. When I first joined Mansfield players would always stay behind for extra training, which was quite incredible really. Frank Wignall, one of the senior and most respected players at the club, would always be willing to give advice and he was so helpful in my early time at Field Mill'.

Bird's career blossomed and the number six shirt became his sole possession. As part of Dave Smith's 'famous back five', with 'keeper Rod Arnold, Sandy Pate and Barry and Colin Foster, Kevin played a major part in the Division Four title success in 1974–75.

Two years later, his eight goals from defence helped clinch the Division Three title under new boss Peter Morris. Kevin still feels that, despite claiming another medal, he was played out of position that season.

'In my opinion Sandy was still the best right-back around, yet Peter wanted me to do a job there. I knew my own strengths and weaknesses and my best position was in the middle. I just felt that we weren't playing our best players in their correct positions'.

Nevertheless, the Stags advanced and spent their only season in English football's second tier, where the going, to be frank, was tough. The Christmas period was particularly hectic but provided a career highlight for 'Birdy'. Having scored at home against Fulham on Boxing Day, Kevin scored the Mansfield goal, just 24 hours later, in a 1–1 draw at White Hart Lane against Spurs.

'I can't remember too much about the goal now', he admits. 'I do seem to think it was one of the most important I scored for the club, accounting for the setting, the occasion, the opposition'.

The majority of his 60-plus goals for the club came from set-plays – by fiercely launching himself at crosses to power home unstoppable headers. Many of his contempories in the Mansfield side allowed their facial hair to flourish – Kevin went the whole way, nurturing a beard to round off the warrior look.

Fittingly he scored on his final appearance for the Yellows, netting in a 3–2 defeat at Peterborough in May 1983. He then joined Huddersfield Town, but the move meant an unwanted disruption to his settled home life so he opted to turn his back on the professional game and play local non-league football instead. Kevin still resides in Mansfield Woodhouse and for many years has worked for a national supermarket chain.

Stuart Boam

Date of birth: 28 January 1948 Kirkby-in-Ashfield, Notts

Mansfield Town record:

Appearances: League 190, FA Cup 16, League Cup 7
Goals: League 4, FA Cup 0, League Cup 0
Debut: 12 May 1967 v Leyton Orient (a) lost 2–4

Manager: July 1981–January 1983

Also played for: Middlesbrough, Newcastle United, Hartlepool United, Guisborough

STUART Boam was an outstanding young central defender, who later returned to the club for an injury-ravaged stint as player-manager. A local lad, Stuart was primarily a midfielder as a youngster. He was switched to the heart of the defence for the Stags 'A' team when the regular incumbent failed to show, and he never looked back.

While just 19, he was thrust into the first team for the final outing of the 1966–67 season. He missed the first couple of league matches at the start of the next campaign but then went more than two years before missing his next game for the Stags.

A tall, commanding figure, he was a powerful header of the ball and a constant threat in the opposition area. Surprisingly, he never managed to score more than one goal a season during his time with Town. For much of his first period at Field Mill results were poor and the side were always close to the wrong end of the table. Stuart's career continued to blossom, though, and it was evident that Mansfield had a hot property on their books.

The nationwide exposure, given to the club for their FA Cup giant-killing exploits, attracted many scouts to Field Mill and eventually Stuart was allowed to move on. He joined Middlesbrough in the summer of 1971 for a fee of £50,000, and under Jack Charlton rose to the position of club skipper. As captain, he led the side into the top flight and went on to make a total of 378 league and cup appearances for the club.

Stuart stayed in the north-east, with a move to Newcastle United, before accepting an offer to rejoin Mansfield Town as player-manager. A back injury disrupted his return and he started only 13 matches in a season and a half. Unable to lead from the front, his first crack at management didn't go well. Attendances were poor and the club only just avoided the need to seek re-election.

Following a boardroom reshuffle Stuart and his assistant, Geoff Allen, were dismissed. Finally clear of injury, Stuart signed on a non-contract basis as a player for Hartlepool United, before moving into the non-league game.

Through little fault of his own, Stuart's reputation at Field Mill was tarnished a little by his stint as manager, but those fortunate enough to have seen him play in his younger days will, quite rightly, recognise what an outstanding defender he was for the club.

Ian Bowling

Date of birth: 27 July 1965, Sheffield

Mansfield Town record:

Appearances: League 172, FA Cup 7, League Cup 9, Others 7
Debut: 12 August 1995 v Fulham (a) lost 2–4

Also played for: Lincoln City, Hartlepool United, Bradford City

IT IS said that you have to be mad to be a goalkeeper. Hardly ever glamorous, it seems every mistake is highlighted and injuries are an occupational hazard. No one who saw Ian Bowling play for Mansfield Town could have cause to doubt his bravery.

His first full season with the club saw him make a total of 50 appearances in both league and cup. He had no real understudy, so when he broke a finger he was forced to strap it up and continue. That was just the kind of commitment that made Ian such a firm favourite with the supporters. On no fewer than three occasions he won the club's Player of the Year awards.

Ian signed for the Stags soon after the departure of Darren Ward to Notts County in 1995. Big and commanding, he proved to be a fine shot-stopper. He relaxed those around him – he was everything a supporter wanted from a goalkeeper.

During the 1996–97 season it was discovered that Bowling had been playing for several months on a week-to-week basis, so it came as a relief when it was announced that he had agreed to sign a contract. His form at the time had been excellent and the promising youngster Nicky Weaver was unable to dislodge him from the starting line-up.

The 1997–98 season progressed nicely for Ian, until October when minor surgery on his elbow went dramatically wrong and his arm swelled to double its normal size. He had to return to hospital.

In an FA Cup tie away at Oldham, Bowling had to perform with his injured arm all strapped up, but said afterwards, 'I was in a lot of pain every time I dived but I wanted to play and didn't want to let the lads down.' That was how he was – always prepared to go the extra mile for his teammates.

Ian made 44 appearances that season but, in a poor piece of timing, was sent off for handling outside his area on the occasion of his 250th league appearance. At the start of the 1998–99 season, Bowling signed a new two-year contract, but again his career was to be blighted by injury. This time he had to play on with a groin injury that was eventually treated in January. He returned to the side in February and rightly won the man of the match award for an outstanding performance in a 0–0 draw against Carlisle United.

There is no doubt that injuries played a major part in the Field Mill career of Ian Bowling. Towards the end of the 1998–99 season he suffered again, breaking his arm in the 1–0 defeat against Exeter City at Field Mill.

After that it seemed as if he never really recovered his full fitness, and it came as no surprise when in the 2000–01 season he was released from the club. The supporters of Mansfield Town will no doubt always remember Ian Bowling with fondness. He was a terrific goalkeeper – but just a little injury-prone!

Donald Bradley

Date of birth: 11 September 1924, Annesley, Notts
Died: 26 June 1997

Mansfield Town record:

Appearances: League 384, FA Cup 25, League Cup 4
Goals: League 6, FA Cup 0, League Cup 0
Debut: 20 August 1949 v Southport (a) drew 1–1

Also played for: Clipstone Colliery, West Bromwich Albion

DON Bradley will, quite rightly, be remembered as one of the most outstanding left full-backs ever to play for Mansfield Town. Over 13 seasons, he compiled 384 league appearances, a club record, which stood until it was overtaken by Sandy Pate some 16 years later.

Born just three miles from Field Mill, Bradley played as a goalkeeper during his younger days and had represented the Dukeries Schoolboys in that position. During the war Don signed for West Bromwich Albion, but didn't make any league appearances for them. He also 'guested' for the Stags in a couple of matches but didn't move to Field Mill until the 1949–50 season, making his debut on the opening day of the campaign.

His first goal for the club came in a 4–0 home thumping of Barrow in his second season with the club, but Don wasn't to become a prolific scorer, netting only five more goals in the next 11 seasons, with two of them coming in the same match, at home to Southport in 1953.

With Don in the number three shirt and Sammy Chessell wearing the number two, the Stags fielded one of their most accomplished and long-standing full-back partnerships in the club's history. Chessell appeared in 275 games for the club and Bradley in a total of 413, with 384 of them in the league. One other league appearance, against Accrington Stanley, was later expunged from the record books after that club folded.

A succession of injuries sidelined Don throughout his career, otherwise his tally would have been even more impressive. On only one occasion, in the 1951–52 season, did he manage to play in every league game.

Don's final game for the club came on 23 October 1961, at the age of 37, when he played in a 2–1 League Cup replay defeat to Cardiff City at Ninian Park. The original tie at Field Mill, which ended 2–2, was an important milestone in the club's history as floodlighting was introduced for the first time.

Initially intending to retire after leaving the Stags, Don then accepted an offer to turn out for Ilkeston Town and he continued his playing career for another couple of seasons.

Colin Calderwood

Date of birth: 20 January 1965, Glasgow

Mansfield Town record:

Appearances: League 100, FA Cup 6, League Cup 4, Others 7
Goals: League 1, FA Cup 1, League Cup 0, Others 0
Debut: 13 March 1982 v Crewe Alexandra (a) won 2–0

Also played for: Swindon Town, Tottenham Hotspur, Aston Villa, Nottingham Forest, Notts County,
Scotland (36 caps)

Managed: Northampton Town

THE Stags knew they'd got a good'un when they spotted Colin Calderwood playing for Ayr United Boys.
He was invited down for a trial and taken on. At the time, Mansfield had a small squad and a run on
injuries and suspensions brought Colin a very early opportunity in the first team, and he made his
debut aged just 17 years and 52 days old.

All round it was a day neither the youngster nor the club would forget. Calderwood's registration
form hadn't been received by the Football League so the Stags were docked two points for fielding an
unregistered player. The match proved to be Colin's only first-team outing that season, but over the
next three campaigns he was given more and more opportunities as his talents began to blossom. He
made exactly 100 league appearances for Town, kicking off a career that was to bring him 36 Scottish
caps and regular top-flight football.

There was plenty of expertise at hand whenever Colin wanted to know more about central
defensive play. His first manager at the club had been Stuart Boam, no mean performer himself, and
then he'd lined up alongside the likes of Billy Ayre and George Foster, two gnarled and gritty war
horses.

'They were my minders', remembers Colin. 'They looked after me and made sure I was doing things
the right way. Another who taught me a lot about the game in those days was Steve Whitworth. I
really enjoyed it when he was playing alongside me, at right-back.'

Most young professionals remember their first goal, but for Colin it's not something he wants to
dwell on. 'I'd headed in a free kick, against Doncaster in the Cup. Straight afterwards I got a knock. It
transpired I'd dislocated the leg bone out of the ankle socket. I was stretchered off but then sent back
on, to run off the injury! By Monday I was in agony and a different perspective was being put on the
injury. I'd ruptured some ligaments and was out for three months.'

Colin joined Swindon Town in July 1985 in a deal that eventually proved to be very good news for
Mansfield. The transfer fee was set at a ridiculously low £27,500 by a tribunal, but with an added sell-
on clause. When the defender joined Spurs for £1.5 million, some eight years later, the Stags received
half the money. The total Calderwood transfer fee eventually worked out at £655,000, a Mansfield
record.

The defender's overdue arrival in international football came at the age of 31, but he played for his
country at the 1996 European Championships and the France World Cup two years later.

Later in his career Colin completed the 'Nottinghamshire hat-trick', having short spells at both
Forest and County, to join a very small band of players who've played for all three of the county's
league sides.

Colin's first season in management ended in disappointment, in May 2004, back at Field Mill. His
Northampton Town side missed out on a trip to the Millennium Stadium for the Third Division play-
off Final, after the Stags pipped them in a penalty shoot-out.

Dave Caldwell

Date of birth: 31 July 1960, Aberdeen

Mansfield Town record:

Appearances: League 157, FA Cup 12, League Cup 13, Others 6
Goals: League 57, FA Cup 4, League Cup 2, Others 1
Debut: 29 September 1979 v Reading (a) lost 0–1

Also played for: Inverness Caledonian, Carlisle United, Swindon Town, Chesterfield, Torquay
United, KV Overpelt (Belgium)

THE END of the seventies signalled the disappearance of the so-called 'Terrace Hero', a particular type of football character, a flamboyant jack-the-lad, idolised by one and all, but who never quite did enough to fulfil his potential. Few of these personalities survived into the early and mid-eighties. They were, sadly, a fading breed as English football hit an all-time low. However, Mansfield Town supporters were granted a reprieve in the shape of Dave Caldwell.

He had joined the club as an eager youngster in June 1979, signing from Inverness Caledonian. Little did anyone know then what kind of impact he would have over the next six years. With his trendy hairstyle, fiery temper and natural goalscoring prowess, he was everything a desperate generation needed and was truly idolised by the supporters.

He never seemed to score simple goals. Dave's trademark was the spectacular. One particular favourite from his goalscoring locker came when he scored a 74th-minute winner in the Freight Rover Trophy Northern Area semi-final away at Bolton Wanderers in 1985. His confidence, bordering on 'cocky', was encapsulated within a few seconds as he rounded the goalkeeper, celebrated before the ball had hit the back of the net and then set about enjoying the moment by leaping onto the fence that was the only barrier separating him from his wild and adoring fans. It was a special moment that none of the travelling Mansfield army will ever forget.

Caldwell seemed to score goals for fun. His own particular favourite came early on in his Stags career, in a 3–1 win away at Mossley in the FA Cup. He ran the length of the field, leaving a couple of defenders for dead, working his way along the byeline before beating the goalkeeper with a left-foot blast that flew into the top corner of the net. Dave admitted later, 'That was the best goal of my career, I beat the whole team, hit it with my left and it went into the top corner. It was unusual to score with my left foot.'

Controversy followed Dave around. In his Stags career alone, he was sent off twice, booked 36 times and suffered an incredible eight suspensions. His goalscoring record spoke for itself – it was just a shame that his disciplinary record interfered with his natural talent, but that was Dave Caldwell and the fans wouldn't have had him any other way.

His best season came in 1983–84, when a Stags side that consistently struggled throughout the season was blessed to have the Scotsman in the side. His 23 goals that season did more than enough to stave off the need to apply for re-election. He scored three hat-tricks, including four goals in a brilliant 26-minute spell at home to Hartlepool United in a 5–0 win.

Caldwell's last-ever game in a Mansfield shirt came in the Freight Rover Trophy Northern Area final defeat at the hands of Wigan Athletic. The Stags lost on penalties, and were denied a place in the Wembley final. Dave left the club soon afterwards to join near-neighbours Chesterfield for £12,000.

He was a hero of a generation, and his like will probably never be seen again.

Raich Carter

Date of birth: 21 December 1913, Sunderland
Died: 9 October 1994, Willerby, near Hull

Mansfield Town record:

Manager: January 1960–January 1963

Also played for: Sunderland, Derby County, Hull City, England (30 caps)
Also managed: Hull City, Leeds United, Middlesbrough

TO FOOTBALL fans of another era, Horatio Stratton Carter was, quite simply, one of the most outstanding footballers of his generation. Born in Sunderland, he made his debut for his home-town club during the 1933–34 season, two months before his 19th birthday. Before he had reached 24 he had achieved everything the game could offer him and was a household name.

A gifted inside-forward, he was quickly elevated into the England team and became the youngest man to captain a Championship-winning side when he led the Roker Park club to the title in 1936, aged just 22.

Despite his prowess in the centre of the park, Raich was also the club's leading scorer and he almost single-handedly ended Arsenal's reign as the country's top side by banging in a hat-trick against them in a thrilling 5–4 win.

He increased his medal collection when he captained Sunderland to FA Cup final glory, scoring the second goal in a 3–1 win over Preston North End. Carter's best years were lost due to the onset of war, but he continued to play for his country in unofficial internationals and he joined Derby County.

When peace returned he played his part in helping the Rams to 1946 FA Cup final glory, becoming the only player to win a medal on either side of the war. The same summer he made his debut in first-class cricket, appearing for Derbyshire.

Carter joined Hull City as player-manager and was instantly rewarded with the Third Division title in 1949. He continued playing until 1953 before ending his career with a tally of 218 goals from 451 appearances, a total that would have been greatly increased but for his war-time inactivity.

Raich then managed Leeds United before taking a short break from the game. He returned to take over at Field Mill in January 1960.

His time in charge of Mansfield brought untold notoriety to the town, encouraging many residents to become aware of football for the first time. Unable to prevent relegation at the end of that first season, Carter introduced new blood into the team and made steady progress before leaving to take over at Middlesbrough in early 1963. Ironically, four months after his departure, the Stags won promotion back to the Third Division.

Carter retired from football in 1966 to run the sports department in a local store in Hull. He suffered a stroke in September 1994 and passed away at his home in Willerby, aged 81.

Keith Cassells

Date of birth: 10 July 1957, Islington, London

Mansfield Town record:

Appearances: League 163, FA Cup 7, League Cup 11, Others 14
Goals: League 52, FA Cup 3, League Cup 3, Others 3
Debut: 17 August 1985 v Hereford United (h) won 4–0

Also played for: Watford, Peterborough United, Oxford United, Southampton, Brentford

LIFE was never uneventful with Keith Cassells around! The very mention of his name brings images of glory, passion and commitment. No one, in the history of the club, could have made more of an impact in both their first and last games at Field Mill.

Keith was 28 when he came to Mansfield, a good age for a striker. He'd learnt the tricks of his trade and was ready to apply them when he joined Ian Greaves's side in the summer of 1985. The statisticians reached for their history books when Keith scored a home hat-trick against Hereford United on his debut. Only Ted Harston in 1935 and Harold Crawshaw, two years later, had achieved a similar feat for the club.

From then on, until his early retirement from the game to join the Hertfordshire Police Force, Cassells could do no wrong in the eyes of the fans. His goals helped the club to promotion that season and a year later he was part of the side that went to Wembley. No one worked harder that day, and Keith literally ran himself into the ground in his efforts. His cross set up Kevin Kent for Mansfield's goal, and although it turned out alright in the end, Keith didn't deserve his subsequent moment of ill-fortune.

Having given his all for the cause, it was heartbreaking to witness his despondency when his kick in the penalty shoot-out was saved. However, the ultimate joy upon his face as the players danced their way around the stadium following Tony Kenworthy's winning penalty, was one of the abiding memories of a jubilant day.

On two occasions Keith was the club's leading scorer and his tally of 52 goals in 163 league appearances stands up to close scrutiny. Apart from his opening day heroics, he hit one other hat-trick for the club, scoring four goals in a 5–0 win over Bristol Rovers.

He marked his final home appearance in unusual circumstances. Having scored earlier in the match, his last-ever action as a Mansfield Town player was to move from up front to play out the last 20 minutes in goal, replacing the injured Andy Beasley. The resounding ovation he received as he left the Field Mill turf for the last time was a fitting testament to a player who would live long in the hearts of all Mansfield Town supporters.

Roy Chapman

Date of birth:	18 March 1934 Kingstanding, Birmingham
Died:	March 1983

Mansfield Town record:

Appearances:	League 136, FA Cup 8, League Cup 6
Goals:	League 78, FA Cup 6, League Cup 4
Debut:	26 August 1961 v Wrexham (a) lost 0–5

Also played for: Aston Villa, Lincoln City, Port Vale, Chester, Stafford Rangers

Managed: Lincoln City, Stafford Rangers, Stockport County

ROY Chapman was an incredibly prolific goal-scorer who was at his peak during his time at Field Mill in the early 1960s. Alongside the emerging Ken Wagstaff, Roy helped form one of the most successful strike partnerships in the clubs' history.

Born in Birmingham, Roy was taken on by Aston Villa as an 18-year-old after shining for the local Kynoch Works team, as he worked in the munitions factory. A five-year stay at Villa Park only produced 19 first-team appearances and eight goals, although he did score on his debut against Middlesbrough.

Roy moved on to Lincoln City and then the Stags, who signed him in August 1961, for £10,000. Boss Raich Carter took an immediate liking to his new hardworking and dedicated professional and Roy rewarded him with 20 goals in his first season with the club.

The following year he was even more productive, with 30 league goals. Incredibly, he was outscored by 'Waggy', who hit 34. Unsurprisingly with that sort of tally, the Stags won promotion to Division Three that season!

Among Roy's haul in that campaign was a league hat-trick against Tranmere Rovers and another in the FA Cup against Hounslow. The non-league minnows were slaughtered 9–2 that day, with Ivan Hollett also scoring three times.

In the next round of the FA Cup that season, the Stags created an unwanted footballing record. Playing away against Crystal Palace, all 10 of Mansfield's outfield players, Roy among them, were cautioned for dissent after disputing a controversial penalty award.

Hat-tricks were becoming increasingly commonplace for the Mansfield front-men of that era and Roy Chapman took his total to four for the club when he achieved two more the next season. Both came at Field Mill, one against Southend United and the other, to claim local bragging rights, against Notts County.

In January 1965 Roy was transferred to Lincoln City, where he later enjoyed a spell as player-boss. As his playing career wound down he had a short stint in charge at Stockport County. Roy's finest managerial achievements came with Stafford Rangers, whom he twice led to Wembley success in the FA Trophy Final.

Tragedy struck in March 1983, when Roy Chapman died from a heart attack while playing in a five-a-side game. His son Lee enjoyed a lengthy and successful career in football, playing for a number of clubs including Stoke City, Arsenal, Nottingham Forest and Leeds United.

Sammy Chapman

Date of birth: 16 February 1938, Belfast

Mansfield Town record:

Appearances: League 155, FA Cup 11, League Cup 3
Goals: League 40, FA Cup 2, League Cup 0
Debut: 18 September 1956 v Southport (a) drew 1–1

Also played for: Glenavon, Manchester United, Shamrock Rovers, Stafford Rangers

Managed: Wolverhampton Wanderers

SAMMY Chapman played over 150 league games for Mansfield Town, helping the club win promotion to the Third Division in 1963. Indeed it was Sammy's goal, away at Stockport, on the final day, which secured the triumph and remains his favourite Stags moment.

'We were losing 1–0 and were in a bit of trouble. I played the ball forward to Ken Wagstaff and carried on running as I knew he'd play it back to me. The pass was perfect and I just drew the 'keeper and slotted it in.'

The point meant that Town went up on goal average, ahead of Gillingham. Sammy, with 40 appearances in midfield, and five important goals, played a major part in an eventful season. He said, 'Defending wasn't our strength but we had lots of players who liked to get forward and score, and we had some quite remarkable matches.'

In 46 league games the Stags scored a total of 108 goals and in the FA Cup they ran amok, beating Hounslow 9–2 and Crystal Palace 7–2.

Sammy had been a Busby Babe – almost literally. 'I came across from Northern Ireland at 14 to join Manchester United. They made me go to school for another year before joining the ground staff. I played for the youth team with the likes of Bobby Charlton, Duncan Edwards and Albert Scanlon.'

In August 1956 Sammy moved to Field Mill, for the first time, under Charlie Mitten. He made 50 league appearances in his first spell with Mansfield and recalls a couple of early goals.

'We were playing away at Bury. I worked out that I could play the game, get a train to Liverpool and be on the night ferry back to Belfast. I asked the manager for permission and Charlie said I could go, if I scored – I made sure, I got two!'

In 1958 Sammy joined Portsmouth but later jumped at the chance to return to Mansfield. 'I was always injured at Portsmouth', he remembers. 'One day, playing away at Sheffield United, I was approached and told that Raich Carter wanted to sign me for Mansfield. I couldn't wait to go back.'

Sammy slotted into a midfield role: 'I sat back in the holding role and allowed Peter Morris to make the forward runs. What a beautiful player he was! Raich really had assembled a very decent side at the time and then Tommy Cummings came and added to it.'

The name of Sammy Chapman will be forever tarnished by his involvement in the 'Fixed Odds' bribery and betting scandal, which ultimately curtailed a successful playing career in 1964. 'That really was the low point of my life', Sammy admitted later. 'I was stupid – naïve really, to get involved. The Lord gives you bits and he tests you – he really tested me. But I managed to bounce back.'

Sammy received a six-month prison sentence but later returned to the game he always loved. In 1985–86 he briefly managed Wolves before becoming one of the game's most respected scouts.

During his time in charge of the England national team, Sven-Goran Eriksson regularly utilized Sammy's talents to watch Premiership games or to travel abroad to spy on foreign opposition.

Steve Charles

Date of birth: 10 May 1960, Sheffield

Mansfield Town record:

Appearances: League 237, FA Cup 12, League Cup 16, Others 13
Goals: League 39, FA Cup 4, League Cup 1, Others 4
Debut: 15 August 1987 v Bristol City (h) won 2–0

Also played for: Sheffield United, Wrexham, Scunthorpe United, Scarborough

THEY say footballers don't have brains, but Steve Charles was the exception – a native of Sheffield, he attended the university there and ended up with a fistful of qualifications and a couple of degrees. As a Mansfield Town player, Steve played his part in a successful promotion campaign in 1992 and he also appeared in two winning Notts FA County Cup final sides.

Football was always an attractive alternative to education and from an early age Steve was tipped for stardom. On Sheffield Wednesday's books as a youngster, he appeared for England Schools at Under-15 level. A deceptively quick midfielder, his game improved at university sufficiently for the red half of his home city to nip in and offer him a full-time contract in January 1980.

Steve won a Division Four Championship medal in just his second season with Sheffield United and became a firm favourite at Bramall Lane. It wasn't just his opponents that needed to brush up on their homework – Steve kept up his studies to collect the first of his degrees, in mathematics. Having compiled over a century of appearances for the Blades he was transferred to Wrexham, where he helped lift the Welsh FA Cup in 1986.

In the summer of 1987 Steve was the only player that Ian Greaves chose to add to his Freight Rover winning squad and he made his debut on the opening day of the new season. Such was the consistency of his performances, that he was an ever-present that season. Wearing the number 11 shirt, he played on the left of midfield but became an increased threat at set-pieces. Many of his league goals for Mansfield came either from the penalty spot or from free kicks.

He rarely missed from the spot – but the day he did might have changed the course of history. Wimbledon's FA Cup triumph of 1988 included a Fourth Round win at Field Mill. The Dons might have gone out but for a fine penalty save by Dave Beasant – something he was to repeat at Wembley.

During his days at Mansfield Steve occupied his spare time doing an Open University course and gained his second degree, in marketing.

One of the unsung heroes of the Town side, Steve carried out the dirty work for the team – tackling back to help the defence and getting forward to support the front men. Hard working and industrious, he gained immense respect from his teammates. During his five years with the club, Steve saw the side drop out of the Third Division, but made sure he was around to help them bounce back.

In November 1992 he went on a short loan spell to Scunthorpe United before signing for Scarborough on a permanent basis. Steve was one of the most well-respected and dignified players to wear the Stags jersey and one who secured his future long before the end of his playing days.

Sammy Chessell

Date of birth: 9 July 1921, Shirebrook, Derbyshire

Mansfield Town record:

Appearances: League 256, FA Cup 19
Goals: League 7, FA Cup 0
Debut: 17 November 1945 v Gainsborough Trinity (h) won 3–0

Also played for: Welbeck Colliery Welfare, Spalding United

SAMMY Chessell's name was among the first to be pencilled on to the Stags team sheet for almost nine years. A great club servant, he was a wonderfully talented full-back, who was equally at home on either side of the defence.

His father had also been a professional footballer, playing for several seasons with Brighton and Hove Albion. Sammy grew up in the Shirebrook area and developed his footballing skills in the Welbeck Colliery Welfare side.

During World War Two Sammy joined Mansfield Town, playing as a forward. Full of running and bursting with enthusiasm, he scored 10 goals in 62 matches. The FA Cup restarted soon after the cessation of hostilities and Sammy's first 'official' matches for Town came in that competition. In two-legged affairs, the Stags overcame Gainsborough Trinity and Grantham Town, before losing 5–0 on aggregate to Sheffield Wednesday in round three. By now Sammy had switched to full-back and, proving his dexterity, he played two of those games at left-back and the other four at right-back.

League competition returned in 1946–47 and the Stags finished bottom of Division Three South. Sammy played in 35 of the 42 matches – no one played more – and scored his first 'proper' goal for the club, on the last day at home to Leyton Orient.

Initially with Dai Jones and later with Don Bradley, Sammy formed reliable and long-standing full-back partnerships – a trend that has continued throughout the club's history.

The only tangible success that Sammy could be associated with during his days with Mansfield Town came at the end of the 1950–51 season when the side finished runners-up in the league. He was one of three ever-presents during that campaign. In addition to their performances in the league that season, the Stags reached the Fifth Round of the FA Cup, going out to Blackpool, the eventual finalists.

Alas, the next season was one of heartbreak and pain for Sammy. On Christmas Day, away at Hartlepools United, he broke a leg. Thankfully he returned towards the end of April, in time for his own testimonial match against Derby County, marking his 10th year with the club.

He continued to play for Mansfield for a further two seasons, taking his tally of league appearances beyond the 250 mark. In August 1954 he ended his association with the Stags by signing for Spalding United.

Sammy never ventured far from his home village of Shirebrook and settled there upon his retirement, working at the local colliery.

Iyseden Christie

Date of birth: 14 November 1976, Coventry

Mansfield Town record:

Appearances: League 153, FA Cup 9, League Cup 6, Others 4
Goals: League 44, FA Cup 2, League Cup 5, Others 0
Debut: 8 February 1997 v Scunthorpe United (a) won 2–0

Also played for: Coventry City, Bournemouth, Leyton Orient

IYSEDEN Christie had two spells with Mansfield Town and on each occasion he left the fans wondering just how good he could have become. Like most strikers he seemed to thrive on confidence – when it was his day, opposition defenders would struggle to contain him. Goals would come in clusters, and as a result, two hat-tricks in particular will never be forgotten.

During a League Cup tie at Field Mill on 11 August 1997, Iyseden enjoyed a purple patch either side of half-time against Stockport County. He scored in the 44th, 46th and 48th minutes of a pulsating contest to record the quickest hat-trick ever hit by a Stag.

His other memorable triple came during his second period with the club. On 1 November 2002 his rapid-fire hat-trick arrived in just 10 glorious first-half minutes. For good measure, he later added the fourth in a 4–2 home victory over Colchester United.

'Izzy' began his career at Coventry City, his home-town club. He made just one first-team appearance for the Sky Blues but enjoyed a more frequent stint during a loan spell at Bournemouth.

During the latter part of the 1996–97 season Coventry lent the young striker out again – this time to Mansfield Town. Eight appearances failed to produce a goal but did persuade boss Steve Parkin to snap him up on a permanent deal during the close season.

Iyseden's long-awaited first league goal arrived on the opening day of the 1997–98 campaign, during a 2–0 win over Hull City. Despite turning in a man-of-the match performance, the youngster blotted his copybook with a late sending-off. That afternoon encapsulated much of Izzy's career to date!

His first full season at Field Mill yielded 14 goals – and two dismissals – leaving fans to wonder whether they were witnessing the arrival of a natural goalscoring genius or an unreliable hot-head.

Those questions remained unanswered as Iyseden produced a return of just nine goals in the following season. With reluctance, Stags agreed to let him join Leyton Orient. There, his one real highlight came when he scored one of the goals in the O's 4–1 FA Cup win away at Portsmouth. Injuries blighted his time at Brisbane Road and so, at the beginning of the 2002–03 season, boss Stuart Watkiss decided to bring him back to Field Mill to join the Stags in the Second Division.

Although it was a season that ended in relegation, Christie hit the headlines by netting 19 league and cup goals – his best-ever return. Among his output that season was a much talked-about equaliser at Meadow Lane. Deep into injury time, and trailing 2–1, Iyseden latched onto a long through ball and fired home an equalising goal that sent the travelling Yellows into raptures.

Under Keith Curle's management Christie again lurched between hero and villain. Two more red cards produced lengthy bans but stunning goals – including another hat-trick, at Southend – took the team to the brink of promotion. Sadly injury ruled Iyseden out of contention for a place at Cardiff for the 2004 play-off final and he was released shortly afterwards.

Ray Clarke

Date of birth: 25 September 1952, Hackney, London

Mansfield Town record:

Appearances: League 91, FA Cup 10, League Cup 7
Goals: League 52, FA Cup 2, League Cup 3
Debut: 17 August 1974 v Southport (h) won 2-1

Also played for: Islington Schools, Tottenham Hotspur, Swindon Town, Sparta Rotterdam, Ajax, FC Bruges, Brighton and Hove Albion, Newcastle United

RAY Clarke was close to being the perfect centre-forward with good all-round technique, strength in abundance and natural goal-scoring intuition. Many lamented the fact that Ray spent a relatively short part of his career at Field Mill, but it was abundantly clear that he was always destined to play at a higher level.

He'd played for England's youth side and scored plenty of goals for Spurs' reserves, before a move to Swindon Town followed. Ray hoped that his career would take off at the County Ground.

'My first season at Swindon was totally disrupted by injuries', he remembers. 'I spent the next summer getting really fit and raring to go. Just a week before our opening match I was called in to see the manager. Danny Williams told me that he'd agreed to let me leave as it was a condition of his move between the two clubs. Whether it was true or not I'll never know but I found myself talking to Mansfield's chairman and manager.'

The move went through and the Stags suddenly realised they'd purchased a player of enormous quality. 'I didn't really know what to expect at Mansfield', says Ray. 'But I loved every minute of my time there. Dave Smith was different class as a manager and we had a great set of lads. There was no animosity between any of us – we all got on well and it showed.'

Ray scored some stunning goals as the Stags marched on to take the Fourth Division title. He feels he could have done even better. 'I played for several weeks when really I shouldn't have done. I'd injured my ankle in a cup tie at Wrexham and then went seven or eight games without scoring but I wasn't fully fit. It was so pleasing to get my fitness back and then the goals returned.'

Playing through the pain barrier enabled 'Clarkie' to become an ever-present in the Championship season, notching 28 goals in the league and another two in the FA Cup. His partnership with Terry Eccles was almost telepathic and destructive as far as opposition defences were concerned.

In his second year at Field Mill Ray netted another 24 league goals, missing just one game all season. His phenomenal strike rate was bound to attract some enquiries, and so it proved.

After two highly productive years with Town, Ray's departure mirrored his arrival. 'I would have been happy to sign a new contract but the chairman told me that the Board had decided, on a split 3-2 vote, to accept an offer for me from Sparta Rotterdam.'

During his time abroad Ray won the Dutch league and cup with Ajax, lining up alongside such seasoned internationals as Ruud Krol, Soren Lerby and Frank Arnesen. Returning to England, he played briefly for Brighton and Hove Albion, and then Newcastle United, before injuries – 'I had three hip operations' – forced a retirement from the game at the age of just 29.

After time spent as a hotelier on the Isle of Wight, Ray Clarke has returned to football, scouting for a number of clubs, including Rangers, Liverpool and Coventry City. He spent the 2003–04 season as Southampton's chief scout.

Wayne Corden

Date of birth: 1 November 1975, Leek, Staffs

Mansfield Town record: (to end of season 2003–04)

Appearances: League 168, FA Cup 9, League Cup 4, Others 7
Goals: League 32, FA Cup 1, League Cup 0, Others 0
Debut: 12 August 2000 v Cheltenham Town (a) drew 2–2

Also played for: Port Vale

WAYNE Corden has provided Stags' fans with some of the most powerful long-range shooting ever seen at Field Mill. His ability to test opposing goalkeepers from all angles and distances ensured that supporters were always kept in a high state of anticipation whenever he received the ball.

Such was the impression he created, he was likened to such stars as Brazilian ace Roberto Carlos for his dead ball destructiveness. Chants of 'Wayn-ho Cordeen-yo' would arise as he lined up free-kick opportunities – a cry that the player simply loved.

Wayne was brought to Field Mill in the summer of 2000. He'd made his mark on Stags boss Bill Dearden, who'd previously coached him at Port Vale. Following his own move to Mansfield, Bill returned to his former club to bag a player who'd shown plenty of potential since his days as a trainee, without fully making the transition into the senior side. In five years as a pro, he'd only made 66 appearances in Vale's league side, incredibly scoring just once.

His first Mansfield goals weren't witnessed by too many. Just 1,447 were at Wrexham to see him score twice – one a howitzer from 30 yards – as the Stags won a League Cup tie 3-0.

Although always playing out wide on the left – Wayne is predominantly right-footed – many a full-back has gambled and lost out as he's torn past them on the outside and whipped in a sublime cross with his supposedly weaker foot.

In Mansfield's promotion season of 2001–02, Wayne was an ever-present, the only member of the side to play in every match. His contribution of eight goals was only beaten by the prolific Chris Greenacre. The following year his tally of league goals was increased to 13. His total could have been higher – four of his goals were from the penalty spot and on several occasions Liam Lawrence took the penalties instead.

In 2003–04 Wayne performed consistently well all season as the side advanced to the play-off final at Cardiff. His aggressive running troubled the Huddersfield Town defence all afternoon and, on more than one occasion, he was within a whisker of breaking the deadlock.

Sadly, his penalty in the shoot-out was one of the unsuccessful ones – but it had been a collective performance to get to the Millennium Stadium and no blame could be apportioned to anyone for losing in such unfortunate circumstances.

Wayne Corden has lit up many a drab game with a sensational piece of opportunism and for that Stags fans will always be grateful!

Tommy Cummings

Date of birth: 12 September 1928, Castletown, nr Sunderland

Mansfield Town record:

Player-manager: January 1963–July 1967
Appearances: League 10, League Cup 1
Goals: League 0, League Cup 0
Debut: 18 March 1967 v Aldershot (h) drew 2–2

Also played for: Burnley
Also managed: Aston Villa

UNLUCKY not to win full England caps as a player, Tommy Cummings had been one of the best centre-halves of his generation prior to joining the Stags as player-boss in 1963. The fact he ended up at Field Mill was down to a couple of phone calls, made just in the nick of time. 'I was down in Bath and about to accept an offer to join them. Someone entered the room while we were discussing the deal and said my wife was on the phone. I went and spoke to Joy who told me that the chairman of Mansfield Town had called to offer me a job there. I made my apologies and left. The Bath offer had been attractive but I was far more interested in joining a league club.'

Injury restricted Tommy to just 11 appearances for Stags, all made within a calendar year of joining the club. 'I shouldn't have been playing at all really', he reflects. 'My knee had about packed up but we just didn't have anyone else to play at centre-half, so on a few occasions I had to give it a go.'

He then decided to hang up his boots for good and concentrate on his managerial role, taking the side to seventh in the table. This should have been much higher as they remained undefeated at home but lost too many games on their travels.

Tommy had to withstand plenty of supporter unrest in November 1964 when it was agreed to sell top scorer Ken Wagstaff to Hull City. A firm fans' favourite, Waggy's departure caused considerable heartache around Field Mill. 'Ken was a great player', says his former manager. 'He really could do it all – make goals, score goals, the lot! We were all sad to see him leave.'

The manager acted promptly, and Tommy signed Bill Curry from Derby County and was rewarded with an abundance of goals. It had been a test of character for the young manager and he had passed with distinction.

Tommy Cummings remained in the Field Mill hot-seat for four and a half years, considerably longer than many of the others that have held the job, either before or since.

In the summer of 1967 Aston Villa persuaded Tommy to join them as their manager. The relationship only lasted 16 months before he was sacked. He later coached abroad and scouted for several clubs, including Burnley, where he had made his name.

He had played in 434 league matches for the Turf Moor club, winning a First Division Championship medal in the 1959–60 season and playing in their losing FA Cup Final appearance of 1962. Still a Clarets hero, Tommy will be found at all Burnley home matches, entertaining sponsors and guests in the hospitality area which bears his name.

Keith Curle

Date of birth: 14 November 1963, Bristol

Mansfield Town record (to end of season 2003–04):

Player-manager: December 2002 – present
Appearances: League 14
Goals: 0
Debut: 14 December 2002 v Blackpool (h) won 4–0

Also played for: Bristol Rovers, Torquay United, Bristol City, Reading, Wimbledon, Manchester City, Wolves, Sheffield United, Barnsley, England (three caps)

MANSFIELD Town have had more than their fair share of player-managers over the years and continued the trend with the appointment of Keith Curle. Like most footballers over the last half century, Keith's move to Mansfield wasn't motivated by the salary.

'I was still on a good playing contract at Sheffield United', he reveals. 'But I felt this was the right move for me at this stage of my career. I had ambitions of moving into management but felt that I still had something to give as a player.'

Having made more than 700 league appearances, in a career which began over 20 years earlier, Keith had the necessary experience to reorganise a Mansfield defence that had been leaking goals at an alarming rate. Taking over in December 2002, he was unable to conjure up the miracle needed to avoid the drop but could see signs of improvement.

'We were something like eight points away from safety when I joined the club', he says. 'All but one of the loan signings had been used up and the season's budget had gone. It was a case of getting on with it.'

Despite the disappointment of relegation, Keith feels that he took some benefit from the closing half of the 2002–03 season. 'It enabled me to grow accustomed to the job and to assess what players we would need to build the club up again.'

Keith has often emphasised his belief in the psychological side of the game. 'It was clear, when I joined, that the players didn't have enough belief in themselves. I can't automatically give them confidence – there's a huge gap between confidence and belief – but I did start to make them feel good about themselves, which is very important.' The 2003–04 season was, ultimately, to end in sadness for the Yellows, but not without the 'Cardiff experience'.

'To lead the team out at the Millennium Stadium was a fantastically proud moment for me', says Keith. 'More than that, it was a day for the people of Mansfield. The fans were terrific and did the whole town proud. Everyone enjoyed having a 'big footballing occasion' to savour. I know that the Chairman was the proudest man in the stadium.'

Words can never truly describe the anguish of a penalty shoot-out defeat, with promotion and the accompanying financial rewards at stake, but Keith feels the side will take some benefit from the occasion. He says 'The season was a long journey. We ended that journey in better shape than we started it and with far more people on board with us. A lot has been learnt which will hopefully make us stronger next time around.'

Injury, and the form of others, restricted Keith to just a handful of playing appearances during his first 18 months at Field Mill but he isn't short of playing memories, in a career which began at Bristol Rovers and has seen him turn out for 10 different league clubs.

'Playing for England in the 1992 European Championships would be the main highlight but I was very proud to join Manchester City from Wimbledon for a £2.5 million transfer fee, a record at the time for a British defender.'

Keith began the 2004–05 season in charge at Field Mill – as the 30th Stags boss since the club joined the Football League.

Bill Curry

Date of birth: 12 October 1935, Newcastle upon Tyne
Died: 20 August 1990

Mansfield Town record:

Appearances: League 102, FA Cup 6, League Cup 4
Goals: League 53, FA Cup 3, League Cup 1
Debut: 6 February 1965 v Grimsby Town (a) 1–1

Also played for: Newcastle United, Brighton and Hove Albion, Derby County, Chesterfield, Boston, Worksop Town, Sutton Town

NO FINER tribute could be paid to Bill Curry than to recall that he was signed to replace Ken Wagstaff. Manager Tommy Cummings acted quickly to snap up Bill for £10,000 from Derby County, after the club's prize asset had been sold to Hull City. Supporter unrest was at a critical stage, for 'Waggy' had been such a popular and successful striker at Field Mill. Cummings, however, knew what he was doing and Bill Curry proved to be an astute and prolific alternative.

Brought up in the north-east, Bill began his career at Newcastle United and, while with the club, he had the distinction of having been involved in, and having scored in, the first league match played under floodlights in the United Kingdom. The match was against Portsmouth, at Fratton Park, on 22 February 1956.

Short, but with pace to burn and an eye for goal, Bill earned England Under-23 recognition during his time at St James' Park. After a season with Brighton and Hove Albion, Bill moved to Derby County in October 1960. For three successive seasons he topped the Rams' goal-scoring charts, so it was quite a coup for Stags fans when he agreed to leave the Baseball Ground for Field Mill.

The newcomer made an immediate impact. In the closing 16 games of the season he netted 15 times, including hat-tricks against Workington and QPR, and four in a 6–1 mauling of Southend United.

Hopes were high when Curry netted twice on the opening day of the next season but it was a false dawn. The club struggled for much of the campaign, although Bill still managed to notch up 14 goals. He led the way again in 1966–67, topping the scoring charts with 22 goals from 45 league appearances.

In the two full seasons he spent with the Stags Bill was the main man – the leading scorer and the one player likely to conjure up the improbable. He developed a cult following among the same fans who had believed that Wagstaff was irreplaceable. During his time at Field Mill he averaged a goal every other game – impressive by anyone's standards!

Bill's playing career was coming to a close when he signed for Chesterfield in 1968, for £2,000. He later joined Worksop Town as trainer, and had spells managing Boston and Sutton Town. He remained in the area after retiring from the game and in August 1990, William Morton Curry passed away at the age of 54.

Billy Dearden

Date of birth: 11 February 1944, Oldham

Mansfield Town record:

Manager: June 1999–January 2002

Played for: Sheffield United, Chesterfield
Also managed: Notts County

MANY Stags fans were reduced to tears when Bill Dearden called time on his reign as Mansfield Town boss. His final game in charge had been a pulsating FA Cup tie against Leicester City. Although the side were narrowly beaten that day, they were in good shape, sitting towards the top of the table and enjoying one of their most successful seasons for some time. Nevertheless, Billy decided to leave Field Mill and take over the vacant managerial hot-seat at nearby Notts County.

Billy was already a well-respected coach when Ian Greaves invited him to join Mansfield Town in June 1984. Popular with the staff and the players, the former striker became an integral part of the club's backroom staff. When Greaves left and was replaced by George Foster, Dearden stayed in the wings and was a driving force behind the Stags' successful promotion campaign of 1991–92.

With footballing management being such an unpredictable merry-go-round, Foster soon made his own exit, and Billy was put in temporary charge while the job was advertised. At first things went well for Billy, who clearly wanted to take on the job on a full-time basis. The Stags drew in his first game in charge and then thumped Scarborough 4–2, but inconsistency, and three heavy defeats, were just around the corner.

Nevertheless, the weeks dragged by with no news of any impending appointment. Billy was settling in to the position and the team steadily rose to 11th in the table. After nine weeks as caretaker-manager he, like most fans, was stunned when the Board announced the arrival of Andy King as the new manager.

Billy accepted an offer from John Rudge to join him at Port Vale. During his first spell at Field Mill he had served as youth team coach, assistant manager and caretaker-manager. In July 1999, after the departure of another Stags manager, Steve Parkin, Billy was at last offered the full-time job as manager at Field Mill. It was an appointment he gratefully accepted. He must have wondered just what he had let himself in for when he arrived at a run-down ground with only nine full-time professionals on the books. The league season began in disastrous style with a 6–0 humiliating defeat away at Brighton and Hove Albion. The whole football club was in need of rebuilding and Billy Dearden set about the task with relish.

Dearden was instrumental in bringing many youngsters through into the first team and was also responsible for the signing of the prolific Chris Greenacre. Billy was laying the foundations and the side were praised from all quarters for their fine attacking football.

In season 2001–02 Billy's side always looked capable of ending a barren decade of football in the basement division. All credit should go to Stuart Watkiss for completing the task, after his appointment as manager when Billy left for Notts County, but the base had been well and truly laid by Billy Dearden and the Stags fans showed their appreciation.

In his new job Billy managed to keep the Magpies in the Second Division, and he struggled to help keep the club afloat during 18 months in administration. But despite these efforts, Billy was sacked by the Notts County board.

During his playing career Billy had been a prolific goalscorer for both Sheffield United and Chesterfield. Despite his Saltergate connections he is one former servant guaranteed a glorious ovation whenever he returns to Field Mill.

Lindy Delapenha

Date of birth: 20 May 1927, Jamaica

Mansfield Town record:

Appearances: League 115, FA Cup 5
Goals: League 27, FA Cup 0
Debut: 23 August 1958 v Southampton (h) lost 1–6

Also played for: Arsenal, Portsmouth, Middlesbrough, Hereford United, Burton Albion,
                   Heanor Town

LINDY Delapenha made many friends during his three-season spell with Mansfield Town. Christened Lloyd, he was always known as Lindy, even by his family, with whom he arrived in England as a youngster, after being born in the West Indies.

During his schooldays Lindy fell in love with football – spending every spare moment kicking a ball. He dreamed of making a career out of the game and was given an opportunity by Portsmouth. After just two seasons and eight appearances for the Fratton Park club, Lindy was transferred to Middlesbrough. This arrangement sat well with both parties – the Teessiders adored Lindy, while the player's response was a decade of honest toil and endeavour. He played 260 times for 'Boro, netting 90 goals in the process.

A managerial change-over at Mansfield in June 1958 heralded Lindy's move to the East Midlands. Charlie Mitten had vacated the manager's hot-seat at Field Mill to move to Newcastle. Sam Weaver, trainer/coach under Mitten, remained behind to take-over his old boss's job. Realising that Town needed strengthening, Weaver made Lindy his first capture.

Hopes were high of a successful campaign – as they so often are for the Stags in August! Those hopes took on a different hue on the opening day of that 1958–59 season. Although Lindy, wearing the number 7 jersey, scored a goal on his debut, Stags were humiliated 6–1, at home, by Southampton, for whom Derek Reeves scored four times.

Delapenha was one of the few successes in what turned out to be a disappointing season. His naturally cheerful Caribbean outlook, combined with a steely determination to succeed, made Lindy popular with teammates and fans alike. Usually playing wide on either flank, he would often respond with a ready quip to the good-natured banter from the crowd.

A tally of nine goals from 39 league starts was a reasonable return from a winger but he bettered it, by one, the following year. Nevertheless, Mansfield suffered relegation to Division Four at the end of the 1959–60 season.

It was to be a similar pattern for Lindy's third and final season at Field Mill. He was steady, the side were poor – as indicated by a final league position of 20th out of 24. After briefly playing non-league football with Hereford United, Burton Albion and Heanor Town, Lindy left the game altogether, to return to the West Indies, where he advanced to a senior position within the Jamaican Broadcasting Corporation.

Craig Disley

Date of birth: 24 August 1981, Worksop

Mansfield Town record (to end of season 2003–04):

Appearances: League 142, FA Cup 10, League Cup 2, Others 5
Goals: League 16, FA Cup 0, League Cup 0, Others 0
Debut: 24 September 1999 v Shrewsbury Town (h) won 4–0

THEY always say blondes have more fun – and Craig Disley certainly appeared to enjoy playing for Mansfield Town. Easily picked out by his distinctive hair colouring, he played a prominent part in one Stags promotion and one big day out in Cardiff.

'The Millennium Stadium experience will live with me forever', he said later. 'To lose the game hurt so much but it was a fantastic feeling to play on such a big stage, in such an important game.'

A Third Division play-off final, against Huddersfield Town, is quite some way from life as a 16-year-old at Retford United, but that's where Craig was spotted and invited to Field Mill for trials.

'Dave Bentley was the youth team manager at the time I started at Mansfield and he was tremendous with us. He was the first major influence on my footballing career.'

Craig's rapid development earned him a first-team place shortly after his 18th birthday, although it wasn't the most nerve-wracking of debuts. 'It was a home match, played on a Friday night, against Shrewsbury Town', he recalls. 'We were coasting at 4–0 so it wasn't as testing as it might have been!'

Sterner tests were around the corner, but 'Dis' was considered 'up for the job' as he cemented a first-team place. He made 24 league appearances in the 2000–01 season and 36 the following year, as the Stags clawed their way out of the bottom flight. 'To achieve promotion with such a young side was quite an achievement, really. I'll never forget the scenes on the last day.'

The young midfielder became a regular on the scoresheet that season, with seven goals in the league. It was the following season that he feels he scored his best for the club.

'Away at Chesterfield – Liam Lawrence knocked the ball in from the right. I brought it down with the outside of my right foot and smashed it home from around the penalty spot. Bearing in mind the opposition, it was a goal I really enjoyed.'

Out of contract at the end of the 2003–04 season, Craig's final game at Field Mill that season couldn't have been more dramatic. 'There were so many emotions in the play-off game against Northampton. We weren't playing that badly but found ourselves 3–0 down. Thanks to Tom Curtis's goal and the penalty shoot-out we made it to Cardiff in the end.'

Stags supporters have been used to seeing Craig dye his hair on occasions – but it's the blonde shades that have usually got preference. He said: 'There's been so much bleach on there at times, I'm surprised it hasn't fallen out yet!'

Whatever the occasion, Craig Disley always made the right impression in a Mansfield Town shirt.

Joe Eaton

Date of birth: 16 May 1931, Cuckney, Notts

Mansfield Town record:

Appearances: League 4
Goals: League 1
Debut: 1 November 1952 v Crewe Alexandra (h) won 3–0

A BOOK about Mansfield Town legends would be incomplete without the inclusion of Joe Eaton. He became one of the most respected administrators within the game, having briefly represented his local club. His modest appearance record would have been greatly increased had injury not terminated his career during 1954.

'I took a kick in the back', he recalls. 'I thought nothing more of it but it continued to give me pain whenever I tried to twist or turn. I saw a specialist in Nottingham and that seemed to cure it for a while but I wasn't able to play again. It's not been an injury that's really troubled me since – it just prevented me from playing football at the time!'

As it was, the young inside-forward only played four times for the Stags first team, netting the winner on his final outing, against Hartlepools United, at Field Mill. Joe remembers the strike: 'It probably wasn't the greatest of goals but one I'll always remember, from six or seven yards out in front of the North Stand!'

Unable to continue as a player, Joe turned to the administrative side of the game, being appointed the club's assistant secretary in 1955 and full secretary the following year, succeeding Herbert N. Mee. Over the next 37 years Joe was to become the longest-serving secretary in Football League history and witnessed many great moments in the fortunes of Mansfield Town. 'The most pleasing thing for me', he reveals, 'is how the club has continued to find so many good youngsters from the local area. It was something that Raich Carter began, all those years ago, and a trend that still continues.'

Joe witnessed many changes at Field Mill and saw many managers come and go. He has a particular fondness for Ian Greaves. 'I thought he was a wonderful man and a terrific manager', says Joe. 'I never thought that in my lifetime I would see Mansfield Town play at Wembley but he helped achieve it. On the way up to Middlesbrough to play the area semi-final he told me, on the coach, that "We could win – with a bit of luck!" I looked at him and knew then that we would do it!'

Fittingly, for a man revered in almost regal terms throughout the game, Joe Eaton watched 'his side' compete in the 1987 Freight Rover Trophy Final from the Royal Box at Wembley Stadium. A more fitting tribute could not have been written. Joe still lives locally and follows the Stags' fortunes with a passion.

Terry Eccles

Date of birth: 2 March 1952, Leeds

Mansfield Town record:

Appearances: League 118, FA Cup 13, League Cup 10
Goals: League 47, FA Cup 8, League Cup 2
Debut: 25 August 1973 v Peterborough United (a) lost 1–2

Also played for: Pudsey Juniors, Blackburn Rovers, Huddersfield Town, Olympiakos (Greece), York City

CLARKE and Eccles, Eccles and Clarke – it didn't matter which way round you talked about them – the fact was, everybody did talk about them. Whether they were the best front two Mansfield have ever paired will be debated long into the future. The simple truth is that, for all-too-brief a period, the Stags had a couple of real goal-machines on the park together.

Terry Eccles is candid about what each of them had to offer. 'I was quick and strong – and would run through a brick wall, if necessary. I was decent in the air and not a bad finisher but it was Ray who had all the skill – he was always around to make things happen and to pick up the pieces.'

Terry joined Blackburn Rovers straight from school and scored six times in 46 appearances for the Ewood Park club. His time there was disrupted by injury, with a broken cheekbone and a broken ankle hampering his progress. 'The ankle happened in a match against Sheffield United. Before the game, our coach Arthur Proudler was really trying to build me up and implored me to make a big impression. I scored and felt great – then after a challenge I looked down and my heel was where my toe should have been!'

Apart from the broken bone, Terry received more pain shortly afterwards. 'I was lying in hospital and Arthur came to visit me. He told me that Liverpool had been interested in signing me to partner Kevin Keegan – but they signed John Toshack instead!'

So instead of Anfield, it was Field Mill, with Stags' boss Danny Williams signing Terry in July 1973 for only £6,000. No one knew then what a good bit of business that would prove to be.

With the club enjoying the most successful period in their history Eccles found his feet – and his head! As powerful a runner with the ball you couldn't wish to see and in full flight he was almost unstoppable. He averaged almost a goal every two games, as the Stags lifted two titles in the space of three seasons. His partnership with Ray Clarke was almost telepathic and one or the other would always seem to be on the scoresheet. Terry hit three hat-tricks for Mansfield Town, against Chester, Stockport County and Grimsby Town – all at Field Mill – no wonder the fans adored him!

Terry's goal tally was helped by him being the side's penalty taker. Not for him a fancy 'dink' over the 'keeper. The Eccles style was a thunderbolt into the roof of the net. 'I didn't miss a single penalty in my whole career – and I lost count of the number I took. That record nearly went against Torquay at Field Mill. I tried to thump it down the middle but it flew off the outside of my boot and screamed into the top corner. It looked great – but I knew how lucky I'd been!'

Huddersfield Town had to fork out a six-figure sum – the first in Stags' history – to prise Terry away from Field Mill in January 1977. Later Terry tried his hand in the Greek First Division with Olympiakos. His final club was York City and he settled in that area.

More than 20 years after their partnership entered Stags folklore, Clarke and Eccles have been reunited. Terry now scouts for Southampton FC, with good friend Ray his immediate boss!

Tommy Eggleston

Date of birth: 21 February 1920, Mitcham, Surrey
Died: 14 January 2004

Mansfield Town record:

Manager: July 1967–July 1970

Played For: Derby County, Leicester City, Watford
Also managed: Ethnikos (Greece), Panahaiki (Greece), Everton

DURING Tommy Eggleston's reign as Mansfield Town manager the club hit the headlines as FA Cup giant-killers. Under his stewardship the Stags knocked West Ham United, with their three World Cup winners, out of the 1968–69 competition. Round six was reached that year, and round five a year later – brief glimpses of success in a period when the club was down on its luck.

Tommy had joined Derby County as an amateur in 1936, turning professional a year later. A wing-half, he only played once in their first team before war interrupted his career. After serving as a Petty Officer in the Royal Navy, he resumed his footballing career with Leicester City and Watford, playing 177 times for the latter over a five-year period.

As trainer, he joined Brentford in 1954 and after similar stints at Watford, Sheffield Wednesday and Everton, he accepted an invitation to succeed Tommy Cummings as the Stags boss in July 1967. Jock Basford was appointed as his assistant, but their first season in charge was one to forget. The side finished in 21st place in the table and were only spared from the drop by the fact that Peterborough United were relegated due to financial irregularities. In addition, somewhat ironically bearing in mind later achievements in the same competition, the side were humbled 5–1 at non-league Tow Law Town in the FA Cup.

Eggleston was possibly fortunate to be given a stay of execution but his second season as Town boss will never be forgotten. The league campaign was nothing out of the ordinary – although a finishing position of 15th was a vast improvement on the previous year.

The first round FA Cup draw was beyond belief – a repeat clash against minnows Tow Law. Lightning didn't strike twice, and the Stags won 4–1. After further triumphs over three Uniteds – Rotherham, Sheffield and Southend – there came a fourth against West Ham United and the most marvellous night under the Field Mill floodlights.

After the star-studded Londoners were beaten 3–0, Tommy praised his team with this great understatement. 'It was a very good display all round. It was an excellent win. The boys really fought well.' The boys fought well in the quarter-final as well, before going out to Leicester City in front of a sell-out crowd.

In the summer of 1970 Tommy was lured away from Mansfield for a financially rewarding stint in Greek football. He returned to join Everton in 1972, initially as youth team coach, but he eventually had a brief stint in charge of the first team.

As a qualified remedial gymnast, Tommy then chose to pursue a career in football physiotherapy and served Plymouth Argyle and Ipswich Town in that capacity until retiring in 1985. Tommy spent his retirement in Tockwith, North Yorkshire. After a stroke in 2001 he battled against illness but died peacefully, in his sleep, on 14 January 2004, aged 83.

Ernie England

Date of birth: 3 February 1901, Shirebrook, Derbyshire
Died: 22 February 1982

Mansfield Town record:

Appearances: League 130, FA Cup 6, League Cup 1
Goals: League 3, FA Cup 0, League Cup 1
Debut: 29 August 1931 v Swindon Town (h) won 3–2

Also played for: Shirebrook, Sunderland, West Ham United, Sutton Town

TO BE strictly accurate, Ernie England is more of a legend among Sunderland die-hards than Mansfield Town fans. But that shouldn't diminish his achievements for the Stags, just emphasise how much of an impression he made in the north-east.

Shirebrook, a Central Alliance club at the time, had nurtured a young local talent and were deserving of the £100 they received when Sunderland nipped in to buy Ernie in December 1919. They would probably feel, on reflection, that they had picked up something of a bargain. Over the course of his nine-season stay at Roker Park 'Mac' England, as he was always known, appeared in 335 first-team games.

A solid and reliable left-back, he played his part during one of the most successful periods in the club's history. Three times they finished third in the top flight and in 1923 they were runners-up. Mac's reputation extended well beyond the north and he gained recognition by appearing in a Football League representative side during 1926. Many feel that he was particularly unlucky not to win full England honours.

He was transferred to West Ham for £500 in October 1930 – five times the amount that Sunderland had signed him for. Mac didn't settle in the capital and yearned to return 'back home'.

His wishes were fulfilled. Mansfield Town were elected to the Football League in the summer of 1931. New players had to be recruited – and quickly! Twenty-three in all were brought in, including Mac, who was signed for £400 from the Hammers.

He will remain in the record books forever as being a member of the first league team fielded by Town and he remained an ever-present during that debut season. Curiously, like Steve Whitworth – another distinguished defender who played for the Stags over 50 years later – Ernie had never scored a single goal until he arrived at Field Mill. Like Whitworth, his debut strike eventually came from the penalty spot, as Ernie's kick earned a draw away at Bristol Rovers.

Ernie England's playing career was put on hold by a cartilage operation during the spring of 1933. Fully recovered, he returned to serve the Stags well until the 1935 close season, whereupon he joined Sutton Town. A year later he was back at Field Mill to spend a short stint as assistant trainer.

Cricket was a big passion of Ernie's life and he played for Langwith Loco during the summer months. He died at Radcliffe-on-Trent in 1982, aged 81.

Wayne Fairclough

Date of birth: 27 April 1968, Nottingham

Mansfield Town record:

Appearances: League 141, FA Cup 5, League Cup 5, Others 10
Goals: League 12, FA Cup 1, League Cup 0, Others 0
Debut: 6 March 1990 v Bolton Wanderers (h) lost 0–1

Also played for: Notts County, Chesterfield, Scarborough

MANSFIELD Town had to equal their record signing fee when they signed Wayne Fairclough from Notts County in March 1990. The £80,000 spent to secure his services matched that forked out to recruit Steve Wilkinson five months earlier.

Few would deny that Wayne was worth every penny. He was another of those professionals to be given the unfortunate 'utility player' tag. It applies sometimes to those players who are just moved about to make up the numbers – this certainly wasn't the case with Wayne Fairclough. He was skilful and adaptable enough to succeed in a number of roles, always accepting the responsibility and never letting the team or his teammates down.

Nottingham-born, he'd made the grade at Meadow Lane, making 71 league appearances for Notts County. His brother Chris, incidentally, split family loyalties by playing over the river at Nottingham Forest and later at Spurs and Leeds United.

George Foster was the Stags boss who signed Wayne and handed him the number 11 shirt for his debut. Over the next four seasons, in the days before squad numbering became the vogue, he would wear every single outfield number.

By any standards 1990–91 wasn't a great season for Mansfield Town and ended in relegation. The performance of one player stood head and shoulders above the rest and Wayne deservedly won the club's Player of the Year award.

A tireless runner who never shunned a tackle, Wayne became a firm favourite at Field Mill for his battling qualities and his 100 percent commitment every time he pulled on the shirt.

Injury forced him to miss the first few months of the next season but he returned, in December, to play a major part in the Stags' successful promotion campaign. He made just 18 appearances but scored crucial goals against Walsall, York City and Crewe Alexandra.

The good times, however, were not to last and the Stags soon faced the drop again. George Foster made way for Andy King and the new boss used Wayne as more of a squad player than a regular starter. Still with plenty to offer, Wayne accepted a bid to move to local rivals Chesterfield, but his two-year stay wasn't entirely successful and included a loan spell at Scarborough in 1996.

After a brief stint with Northwich Victoria, Wayne established himself in the local non-league scene, performing with great distinction for Ilkeston Town and Hucknall Town.

Gary Ford

Date of birth: 8 February 1961, York

Mansfield Town record:

Appearances: League 88, FA Cup 2, League Cup 4, Others 4
Goals: League 7, FA Cup 0, League Cup 0, Others 0
Debut: 23 March 1991 v Shrewsbury Town (h) won 2–1

Also played for: York City, Leicester City, Port Vale, Walsall, Telford United, Lillestrom (Norway), Hartlepool United

THERE is no more uplifting sight for a football fan than to see a winger running at his full-back. When Gary Ford was at his best, he was worth the admission money alone.

Not since the halcyon days of Jimmy McCaffrey had the Stags really possessed a wide player who was capable of the unpredictable. That changed when Gary moved to Field Mill.

It seemed that every time the side attacked the Quarry Lane End of the ground, the West Stand would remain in a state of high anticipation. There, in front of them, was a football being dribbled by a whippet!

In truth, Gary must have lost a yard or two of pace by the time he joined Mansfield. He was in his 30s, and had countless whacks across the shins from beleaguered defenders. Nevertheless, he illuminated Field Mill for a couple of years.

Gary had first made the grade at his local club, York City. He'd joined as a young apprentice in 1977 and signed professional forms in February 1979.

Over the next eight years he was to make over 400 first-team appearances for the Minstermen, 366 of them in the league. During the 1983–84 season he claimed the only medal of his career, with York winning the Fourth Division title.

A fee of £25,000 took him to Leicester City in 1987 but after just six months he was transferred to Port Vale. As at most of his other clubs, he was a firm favourite at Vale Park. In the move that took Kevin Kent the other way, Gary joined the Stags in March 1991. He scored his first goal for the club a month later, in a home draw with Leyton Orient.

It was clear, though, that his talents lay more in providing than scoring. The following season he was the main supply line for Phil Stant and Steve Wilkinson as Town gained promotion. The front two scored 40 goals between them in the league, with Gary topping the table of 'assists'.

He spent a further season at Mansfield before trying his luck in Norwegian football. The experience was brief and he rejoined his old Stags boss George Foster at Telford United.

Gary made three appearances for Hartlepool United in September 1996, taking his overall league tally of appearances to 561.

Tony Ford

Date of birth: 14 May 1959, Grimsby

Mansfield Town record:

Appearances: League 103, FA Cup 4, League Cup 4, Others 6
Goals: League 7, FA Cup 1, League Cup 1, Others 0
Debut: 28 October 1996 v Scarborough (a) lost 1–2

Also played for: Grimsby Town, Stoke City, Sunderland, West Bromwich Albion, Bradford City, Scunthorpe United

THE physical demands of the modern game mean that it is now something of a rarity for a player to stretch his career to almost two decades. One footballer who broke the trend, as well as setting an appearance record, was Tony Ford. Between 1975 and 2002 he played in more Football League matches than any other outfield player in the history of our domestic game.

When Tony joined Mansfield Town, many failed to realise that he was on the cusp of breaking the record. He'd seemingly been around forever – having joined his local side, Grimsby Town, as an apprentice and appeared in the first team in 1975. In almost a decade with the Mariners Tony made more than 400 first-team appearances.

Usually appearing on the right flank, Tony was a capable pro, a good club man and a big favourite with the fans. He played his part in a Division Three title-winning season in 1979–80 but comparative successes were few and far between. Later he appeared in a couple of B internationals for England, one of the high spots of his career.

After a short loan spell at Sunderland, Tony moved to Stoke City in 1986 and then on to West Bromwich Albion three years later. At each of these he clocked up more than a century of league appearances. His tally began to rise but his career looked to be drawing to a close as he switched clubs with increasing regularity.

A second spell at Grimsby was followed by stints at Bradford City and Scunthorpe United. Then it looked to be all over when he accepted an offer to join non-league Barrow. At around the same time Steve Parkin had taken over as player-manager at Field Mill. He had been a teammate of Tony's at both Stoke and West Brom and the two had remained friends. Parkin needed a coach – and Ford responded, and was especially delighted to accept a playing contract as well.

No longer possessing the pace of his younger days, Tony was, nevertheless, of considerable worth to the Stags in a playing capacity. His knowledge helped nurse some of the younger players and his commitment couldn't be faulted. As at all of his other clubs he impressed – and his appearance tally continued to climb.

On 4 January 1998, in a home match against Rochdale, Tony made his 900th first-team appearance and just a year later he smashed Terry Paine's Football League record. The historic day was 16 January 1999, away at Plymouth Argyle. Fittingly, both the Plymouth Argyle players and the rest of the Stags' side lined up to applaud him onto the field of play for that record-breaking feat. Aged 39, Tony Ford was playing in his 825th league match.

In June 1999 Steve Parkin resigned from his position as Stags manager. He accepted an offer to join Rochdale and his right-hand man, Tony Ford, moved with him. Tony had made over 100 league appearances for the Stags, scoring seven times.

He continued his playing career at Spotland, eventually retiring in 2002 with an appearance total of 931 games. Only goalkeeper Peter Shilton has played more.

Barry Foster

Date of birth: 21 September 1951, Langold, Worksop, Notts

Mansfield Town record:

Appearances: League 287, FA Cup 22, League Cup 18
Goals: 0
Debut: 4 September 1971 v Plymouth Argyle (a) lost 1–3

Also played for: Boston United

THEY tell youngsters to 'get your qualifications first'. Barry Foster followed that advice, completing an apprenticeship as a mining electrician at Steetley Colliery before signing professional forms. However highly they rated young Barry at the colliery, they weren't to see him again as he embarked on a career that would see him spend a decade as the Mansfield Town left-back.

After shining in school football in the Worksop area, Barry graduated through the Stags' junior sides, playing youth football for his country along the way. His debut for Mansfield's first team came during the 1971–72 season, just a few weeks before his 19th birthday, ironically on the same day as his unrelated namesake Colin.

Initially Barry had to bide his time, with opportunities at left-back being limited due to the consistency of Clive Walker. Eventually though, Barry Foster took over as first-choice left-back and made the position his own. Short and stocky, he sported the in-vogue long sideburns for much of his professional career and was respected by the Field Mill faithful for his tenacity and courageous tackling.

He appeared 40 times in the side that won the Fourth Division Championship in the 1974–75 season, one of eight players to appear in as many league matches during that campaign. His partnership down the left flank with Jim McCaffrey is fondly recalled to this day, but Barry knew his limitations and responsibilities and rarely ventured too far forward. In 287 league games for the club he didn't register a single goal.

Any doubts about his ability to take a step up in class were soon dispelled as he made 39 starts in the Third Division title-winning side in 1976–77. Joy turned to sorrow when he broke a leg against Portsmouth on the day that promotion was confirmed. The injury ruled him out for the first part of the club's Division Two campaign the following year, but he returned in December to see out the final 25 games of the season.

More than 10 years after his debut, and while still a regular selection, Barry was released, aged 31, to join non-league Boston United. He had worn the Stags jersey a total of 327 times in Football League, FA Cup and League Cup ties, as well as in a handful of appearances in the Anglo-Scottish Cup, Watney Cup and the Notts FA County Cup, winning that event in 1972.

After retiring from the game Barry joined the family market-trading business – rejecting the opportunity, once and for all, to become a mining electrician!

Colin Foster

Date of birth: 26 December 1952, Nottingham

Mansfield Town record:

Appearances: League 205, FA Cup 17, League Cup 10
Goals: League 17, FA Cup 2, League Cup 0
Debut: 4 September 1971 v Plymouth Argyle (a) lost 1–3

Also played for: Peterborough United, Corby Town, Kings Lynn, Stamford

YOU just didn't mess with Colin Foster. No centre-forward relished the prospect of a physical battle against the Mansfield defenders of the mid-1970s. Not among the tallest around, but tough as teak, Colin was a hugely influential member of the Stags back four – solid in defence and always a threat in the opposition's penalty area.

His association with the club began as a 15-year-old schoolboy and he later skippered Town's youth team to the Midland Intermediate Championship. Ironically, he made his first team debut, at the age of 18, in the same match as namesake Barry Foster. 'The question we were both asked, more than any other', says Colin, 'was "Are you brothers?" In the end we both began to admit to strangers that we were – it was easier than trying to explain!'

The Division Four title triumph in 1974–75 should have been a career highlight, but the passing years haven't let a feeling of disappointment slip by. 'I'd played in every one of the first 42 league games and promotion had been secured. I really wanted to remain an ever-present and play in the last four matches but manager Dave Smith had just signed another central defender, Laurie Madden, and wanted to have a look at him.'

Two years later he was part of another Championship-winning Mansfield team and admits to enjoying that success even more. 'I felt that I made more of an impact that season. I scored nine times in the league, as well, and every goal either won us the game or clinched a point.'

Colin recalls that his most memorable goal for the club came in the same match as the most bizarre incident he can ever remember. 'We were playing Gillingham at home. They took a quick free-kick, lofting the ball into our area. While the ball was in the air we all heard the referee blow his whistle. Barry Foster caught the ball but the ref had decided to let play go on and gave them a penalty.'

Later in the same game came a rather more cherished memory. 'I played the ball out to Gordon Hodgson and just kept running forward. Hodgy picked me out with a lovely cross and I just threw myself at it, scoring with a diving header from the edge of the box. I was quite pleased with that one!'

Despite his fearsome reputation, Colin's disciplinary record wasn't that bad, but one sending-off does spring to mind. 'A chap called Fletcher of Burnley threw a punch at me. I wasn't having that, so I gave him one back and he went down like a sack of spuds. Incredibly, I'm sure the ref was just going to tick us both off but then Fletcher started bad-mouthing me and the ref, so we were both dismissed.'

Colin later played for Peterborough United, before doing the rounds of several non-league clubs as player-boss. He settled in the Peterborough area and now works as a painter and decorator. Son Stephen also played for Mansfield Town, during the 1993–94 season.

George Foster

Date of birth: 26 September 1956, Plymouth

Mansfield Town record:

Appearances: League 373, FA Cup 19, League Cup 22, Others 34
Goals: League 0, FA Cup 2, League Cup 0, Others 1
Debut: 27 August 1983 v Bristol City (a) lost 0–4
Manager: February 1989–September 1993

Also played for: Plymouth Argyle, Torquay United, Exeter City, Derby County

IN EVERY sense, George Foster was a colossus for Mansfield Town. Players and fans alike looked up to him and respected him. It is no wonder then, that this lion-hearted defender was the first choice to become the Stags manager when Ian Greaves decided to leave Mansfield Town.

By that time George had been with the club for five and a half years after joining from Derby County for a cut-price fee. In his first season he had been voted Player of the Year and in his second campaign he marshalled a defence that conceded just 38 goals in the league – a club record for meanness!

Leading by example, Foster proved to be an inspirational captain and led the side to promotion in 1985–86 and to Freight Rover Trophy glory at Wembley in 1986–87. Apart from his defensive supremacy, George was always a handful in the opposition area, although he hadn't quite made it as far as the visitors' box when he scored his most spectacular goal in Stags colours.

Having had the misfortune to put through an own-goal earlier, against Wigan Athletic in a Freight Rover Trophy Northern Area Final, and with the match deep inside stoppage time, George unleashed a thunderbolt from 25 yards that literally flew into the top corner of the Wigan net. The goal was special, the celebrations even more so.

The Stags eventually lost that tie but Freight Rover glory was to come their way and no one will forget the look of sheer pride on George Foster's face as he walked up the famous steps at Wembley stadium to collect the Trophy in 1987. It is one of the most enduring memories any Mansfield Town fan will have.

George's appointment as player-manager in February 1989 met with universal approval. A topsy-turvy period in the club's history followed – relegation, promotion, relegation.

How sad that George's association with the club should end on a low. For more than a decade he had given his all for Mansfield Town but in September 1993 that counted for nothing as he was relieved of his position, only to bounce back immediately with his appointment as manager of Conference side Telford United.

Still a highly respected coach in the game, George can fall back upon the experience gained in a total of 649 league appearances. He has many memories of his time at Field Mill – and so do the fans. Thanks George!

Paul Garner

Date of birth: 1 December 1955, Doncaster

Mansfield Town record:
Appearances: League 110, FA Cup 4, League Cup 0, Others 21
Goals: League 8, FA Cup 0, League Cup 0, Others 0
Debut: 15 September 1984 v Crewe Alexandra (h) lost 0–1

Also played for: Huddersfield Town, Sheffield United, Gillingham

PAUL Garner was one of Mansfield Town's Wembley wonders. Left-back that day, he was equally at home in midfield and clocked up a total of 450 Football League appearances before knee injuries forced him to retire in 1989.

His career, which was monopolised by lengthy spells at Huddersfield Town and Sheffield United, ended with a taste of the limelight. Paul had won England youth caps in his early days and claimed a Fourth Division title at Bramall Lane, but his days at Field Mill helped add a touch of gloss to recall in his retirement.

Yorkshire-born, he'd joined Huddersfield at 17 and made 96 league appearances for the Terriers before joining the Blades in November 1975. He became a regular at United for almost nine seasons until his move to Mansfield.

A short loan spell at Gillingham indicated that his days in the steel city were numbered and Ian Greaves leapt at the opportunity to bolster his squad with some proven experience. It looked as if Paul would have to wait a while to claim a win bonus with the Stags but, after three draws and three defeats, he emerged as an unlikely match-winner with his first goal for the club, which was enough to see off Torquay United.

However, 1985–86 began badly for Paul. Injured, he missed out until November but returned to add some bite as the Stags secured a third-place finish. He appeared in just half the matches the following year but remained a key member of the squad and picked up his just desserts the following year, as Mansfield Town began their march to the Venue of Legends.

Paul's own bid to reach the Wembley showpiece almost ended at the Northern Area Final stage. Away against Chester City, he was hospitalised after an early challenge left him with a double fracture of the cheekbone. His injury forced him to miss eight league matches but he returned to play once before the big day itself. On 24 May 1987, Paul Garner played his part in one of the major days in the club's history.

On the field for the whole 120 minutes, he was thankful that he didn't have to take one of the sudden-death spot-kicks at the end and his relief was evident in the celebrations with his joyous teammates.

The Stags were able to celebrate another success with a win over Notts County in the final of the Notts FA County Cup in August 1988, but Paul's injury woes reappeared as he limped out of the action after just six minutes. Over the course of the next 18 months, Paul was beset by a succession of knee problems. He played his last game for the club as a substitute, at Wolves, in December 1988.

Shortly afterwards he bade farewell to the professional game to start life in the insurance business but he later switched occupations by purchasing his own milk round.

Ian Greaves

Date of birth: 26 May 1932, Shaw, near Oldham

Mansfield Town record:

Manager: February 1983–February 1989

Played For: Manchester United, Lincoln City, Oldham Athletic
Also managed: Huddersfield Town, Bolton Wanderers, Oxford United, Wolves

WHEN Ian Greaves took over as Mansfield Town manager in February 1983, there were few who had any idea just what kind of an impact he would eventually have. Greaves, a former 'Busby Babe', was one of the game's big names, and it surprised many that he took the challenge of turning around the fortunes of the small north Nottinghamshire club. 'People asked me why I'd joined Mansfield', he relates. 'It was simple – I needed a job!'

The club weren't going through a particularly successful period and Ian was lured in by false promises. 'The chairman told me I could have whatever money I needed for new signings. A few months later he told me that he was skint!'

Just how badly off the club had become can be qualified by two incidents in particular, which Ian recalls. 'The club paid for the petrol in my car. I used to fill up from the same place every week but one day they refused to serve me as the account was so overdue. On another occasion we had eaten a pre-match meal at a hotel in Peterborough. The head waiter came to me with a bill for £150, saying he wanted paying as the club still owed money from the previous season's visit!'

Far from quitting, Ian accepted the situation and embarked on a wheeler-dealer campaign to bring players to the club, most of whom were far from the finished article. 'At no point in my career did I have to spend so much time on individual, one-to-one coaching.'

Eventually though, the corner was turned. There was a promotion to savour and the Freight Rover Trophy win to celebrate. 'The promotion campaign was the greater achievement, as it was achieved very much against the odds with a side that had been put together in a relatively short space of time. Wembley was a great occasion for the whole town – I was so proud to lead the side out that day. I'd played in an FA Cup Final for Manchester United there but it was extra-special to lead my own team out.'

Ian's successes with the Stags were fully deserved in a career perhaps saved by fate. Somehow he was destined not to die in the Munich air disaster of 1958. 'I had my bags packed to fly out with the rest of the United team. Two days before we were due to go I was told that they were taking Geoff Bent as left-back instead. Naturally I was upset at the time – and Geoff, like so many others, didn't come back.'

In February 1989, following a 2–1 defeat against Notts County, Ian decided to call time on his reign at Field Mill, stating that 'six years was as long as he would serve any club.' Ian Greaves achieved so much at Mansfield Town. He earned the respect and admiration of everyone who worked for him and everyone who met him. The fans will never forget how he helped turn around their club.

Chris Greenacre

Date of birth: 23 December 1977, Halifax

Mansfield Town record:

Appearances: League 121, FA Cup 5, League Cup 2, Others 3
Goals: League 49, FA Cup 6, League Cup 2, Others 0
Debut: 6 November 1999 v Lincoln City (h) won 5–2

Also played for: Manchester City, Cardiff City, Blackpool, Scarborough, Stoke City

CHRIS Greenacre simply loved playing at Field Mill. Even before he joined the Stags it was something of a lucky ground for him, as he scored there in loan spells for both Cardiff City and Scarborough. It was no real surprise then when he continued to find the net, on a regular basis, after joining the Yellows. 'I think there was something of a feel-good factor about me playing at Mansfield', he recalls. 'I was always confident about doing well there and that was a factor in my move from Manchester City.'

Typically, the willo-the-wisp striker netted twice on his Mansfield debut as his love affair with the Field Mill fans began in earnest. 'The supporters were absolutely awesome in the way they treated me', he says. 'I expected them to be a little wary at first but they were truly magnificent towards me. It's something I'll never forget and I just hope they feel I repaid them for their support.'

After a 12-game loan spell Chris joined the club, on a permanent basis, from Manchester City and doesn't regret making the switch. 'I wouldn't change a single thing about my time with the club. I definitely feel it was a good move for my career, Billy Dearden was different class as a manager and the icing on the cake was winning promotion.'

There's little doubt that Chris will always be remembered for his role in that 2001–2002 promotion-winning side. His 21 goals in 44 league appearances were a significant factor in the success. 'Greeny' possessed fine dribbling ability, a powerful long-range shot and was an aerial threat, but his greatest asset, as a striker, was his uncanny ability to sniff out a half-chance.

'I think I just had the happy knack of being in the right place at the right time', he modestly reflects. 'My job is to hold the ball up, give it to a teammate and try to get on the end of things in the box.'

It was no real surprise that the first senior hat-trick of Chris's career came at Field Mill, against Halifax Town, in September 2000. That was just a prelude to the great achievements of the following season.

Those 21 goals in the league, and 28 in all competitions, set up the Stags for a terrific campaign, topped off by the celebration of promotion to Division Two. The season featured another triple, this time against Huddersfield Town in the FA Cup.

Interested clubs had been queuing to sign Chris all season but he saw out his contract, leaving in the summer of 2002 to join Stoke City.

Ian Hall

Date of birth: 27 December 1939, Sutton Scarsdale, Derbyshire

Mansfield Town record:

Appearances: League 145, FA Cup 10, League Cup 4
Goals: League 10, FA Cup 3, League Cup 0
Debut: 1 December 1962 v Newport County (a) drew 1–1

Also played for: Derby County, Derbyshire County Cricket Club

IAN Hall was one of the last true all-round sportsmen. By summer he wore his cricket whites and in winter he earned his living playing professional football. To a certain degree he was fortunate when picking his clubs. 'When I joined Derby County the manager was Harry Storer, who'd played cricket for Derbyshire – and it was Raich Carter who took me to Mansfield – he'd also played a few games for the same county.'

His bosses' tolerance of a dual sportsman was, therefore, perhaps greater than that of most other managers. 'The seasons were slightly different then', says Ian. 'Cricket didn't begin until the end of May and football didn't start until the end of August. The biggest problem was always missing pre-season training and having to catch up on my own.'

In moving to Mansfield after three years with the Rams, Ian had moved full circle. Brought up in Glapwell, he'd attended Brunts Grammar School and set an early record by playing football for Mansfield schoolboys Under-15 side, while aged just 12. He also played at Wembley for England Schoolboys in front of 95,000 fans and played in the same England youth team as Bobby Moore.

He remembers his time at Field Mill with affection. 'When I first joined the club we had a decent side. Ken Wagstaff and Peter Morris were always going to be very good players.'

A gifted batsman for Derbyshire, Ian modestly assesses his impact on the 90-minute game. 'I played either inside-forward or wing-half – it's called a midfield role nowadays – but I tried not to find myself in either penalty area!'

Despite his close affinity to the two clubs he played for, Ian confesses to being a 'closet' Sheffield Wednesday fan. As such, he has no doubt about his favourite match in a Stags shirt. 'In February 1967 we played a Fourth Round FA Cup tie against Wednesday, at Hillsborough, in front of 49,000 people. Although we lost 4–0 it was definitely one of the highlights of my career.'

In his first season with Mansfield Town, Ian enjoyed promotion from the Fourth Division. Two years later, they came close to going up again. 'We missed out on goal average then but it was the congested Easter programme that did us. We beat Hull City on the Saturday and Carlisle United on Easter Monday, at home. The following day we had to drive up to Carlisle for the return match. Unsurprisingly, we lost!'

In April 1967 Ian severed his Achilles tendon while playing for the Stags at Swindon and sampled some classic football humour. 'While I was being carried away on the stretcher, a young lad leaned over and said, "What's up mate, are you tired?"'

Since hanging up his bat and boots Ian Hall has continued to follow both football and cricket, as an eloquent and popular radio summariser, but he yearns for a warmer climate and plans to move to Spain in February 2005.

Edwin Harston

Date of birth: 27 February 1907, Monk Bretton, near Barnsley
Died: 1971 in Rochester, Kent

Mansfield Town record:

Appearances: League 70, FA Cup 3, League Cup 2
Goals: League 81, FA Cup 4, League Cup 0
Debut: 19 October 1935 v Southport (a) drew 3–3

Also played for: Sheffield Wednesday, Barnsley, Reading, Bristol City, Liverpool, Ramsgate Town

EDWIN Harston seems destined to remain in the Mansfield Town record books forever. During the 1936–37 season Edwin, or Teddy as he was known, scored a mind-boggling 55 league goals! His feat was achieved in the old Division Three North and one of football's great coincidences is that Joe Payne, of Luton Town (and once of Bolsover Colliery), scored the same number of goals in Division Three South that very same season!

By his own admission, Teddy came alive in the penalty area – more specifically inside the six-yard box. Getting involved in the build-up or coming deep to look for the ball were alien concepts. As a finisher, though, we've rarely seen his like.

Mansfield knew what they were getting when they signed him– he'd once scored six against them for Barnsley, in a Yorkshire Midweek League game. Hailing from south Yorkshire, Teddy had played for four other clubs before joining Town in October 1935. Bristol City were paid £250 for his services – a quite considerable sum in those days.

Haig Avenue, Southport, has witnessed many outstanding performances over the years. It's doubtful if any other visiting player has ever recorded a hat-trick there on his first appearance for a club. Yet that is precisely what Teddy did, netting all the Stags goals in a 3–3 thriller.

In that first part season with Mansfield, the goal machine churned out a tally of 26 strikes from 29 appearances to easily top the club scoring charts. His second season at Mansfield was simply the stuff of fairytales. His total haul of goals was 58, including a hat-trick in the FA Cup against Barrow. In all, he scored three or more on eight occasions during the season, with a four, two fives and an astonishing seven goals in an 8–2 win over Hartlepools United.

Ted possessed an accurate and powerful shot with both feet and was strong in the air as well. The striker always paid tribute to the excellent service he received from wingers Charlie Rattray and Jack Roy, who provided a good many goalscoring opportunities for him.

It was always likely that he wouldn't remain at Field Mill for long and in June 1937 he signed for Liverpool, for £3,000. Whether he would have been so prolific at Anfield is open to debate, for after a tally of three goals in five games he broke a leg. On returning to full fitness he was confined to the Reds' reserve side and moved into management at non-league Ramsgate Town.

On the face of it, Teddy Harston was a flash in the pan – a one-and-a-half season wonder – but his achievements for Mansfield Town will never be forgotten.

Bobby Hassell

Date of birth: 4 June 1980, Derby

Mansfield Town record:

Appearances: League 160, FA Cup 9, League Cup 7, Others 4
Goals: League 3, FA Cup 0, League Cup 0, Others 0
Debut: 20 September 1997 v Chester City (h) won 4–1

WITH Bobby Hassell at right back – and Liam Lawrence in front of him – the Stags side that went to the Millennium Stadium in May 2004 boasted one of the best right-sided combinations in the country. 'We got on well, on and off the pitch, and felt, as a pairing, we were as good as any around', says Bobby.

Joining the Stags as a youngster, from local league football in Derby, Bobby certainly didn't expect to end up as a full-back. 'More often than not, I'd played as a sweeper in a back three.'

During his younger days at Field Mill he was nearly poached by one of the big boys. 'George Foster, the former Mansfield manager, was scouting for Newcastle at the time and arranged for me to go and have a week-long trial up there. They thought I was a centre-half – so it was no surprise when nothing came of it.'

In September 1997 he made his first-team debut at home to Chester City, as a 64th-minute substitute, with the side already 3–1 up. The following week he made his first start, away at Feethams, in a 0–0 draw against Darlington. His first goal for the club didn't arrive until October 1999, the highlight of a disappointing loss at home to Hartlepool United. 'I received the ball from Darrell Clarke and hit a left-footed curler into the top corner, from about 25 yards. I don't get many goals but they all seem to have gone in with my left foot.'

Bobby's emergence as a first-team regular at Field Mill saw him utilised in either his old position, as sweeper, or in the middle of the park, but it was a switch in formation that saw his conversion to full-back. 'It wasn't until Billy Dearden became manager that I moved to right-back. He said he wanted to change to a flat back four with me on the right.' The switch worked wonders – Bobby swept the board with the Player of the Year Awards as the club celebrated promotion. 'It really was a season to remember for the club and for me individually.'

Out of contract at the end of season 2003–04, Bobby ended the campaign by playing in his biggest match up to that point. 'To play at Cardiff was such a fantastic experience but to end up losing on penalties was definitely the lowest I'd felt during my career.'

The defeat and subsequent failure to clinch promotion prompted Bobby to accept an offer to sign for Barnsley but his relationship with the Mansfield Town fans is something that he'll never forget. 'Throughout my time with the club the fans were really supportive. I'll always appreciate the way they backed me and encouraged me.'

Kevin Hitchcock

Date of birth: 5 October 1962, Custom House, London

Mansfield Town record:

Appearances: League 182, FA Cup 10, League Cup 12, Others 20
Debut: 10 March 1984 v Colchester United (a) lost 0–1

Also played for: Nottingham Forest, Chelsea, Northampton Town, West Ham United

MANSFIELD Town's heroic Freight Rover Trophy-winning goalkeeper was Kevin Hitchcock. When the Stags' Wembley Final of 1987 went down to a penalty shoot-out, it was 'Super-Kev' who delivered, saving crucial kicks from both Gordon Owen and David Moyes.

Yet just 24 hours earlier, while his teammates were walking around the Venue of Legends and getting their first sight of the home of English football, Kevin was an absentee. 'My best mate, Martin Shepherd, had asked me to be the best man at his wedding, due to take place the day before the final', he reveals. 'I didn't think it would be possible but, after winning the semi, I went to see Ian Greaves, the manager, and he allowed me to do it.'

Quite rightly, Kevin will forever be associated with the Stags' glorious day out in the North London sunshine, but he has plenty of other memories from his time at Field Mill. 'I feel really lucky to have had four such good years at Mansfield', he reflects. 'Ian Greaves was a fantastic manager – a real pleasure to play for – and we had a group of lads who would always work hard for each other. The spirit and atmosphere, within the dressing room, was incredible.'

His first professional club had been Nottingham Forest, who had spotted the potential when seeing the youngster playing for Barking. A loan spell at Field Mill in March 1984 enabled 'Hitch' to gather some useful first-team experience. He remained until the end of that season and then joined on a permanent basis.

Apart from the Freight Rover glory, Kevin tasted other success during his time with Mansfield, winning promotion from Division Four in 1985–86. In all, he kept goal for Stags in 224 first-team matches before a transfer fee of £250,000 took him to Stamford Bridge to join Chelsea in March 1988.

Although very much part of the Blues success over the following decade, Kevin often suffered the frustration of being the back-up goalkeeper on many of the big occasions.

Twenty years after making his league debut Kevin is still on call to add to an impressive appearance tally. He spent the 2003–04 season at Watford as goalkeeping coach and twice took his place on the bench as emergency cover.

Despite his long association with Chelsea, Kevin admits there's one result he always looks for first. 'I still follow Mansfield's fortunes. We have family in the area, so I get back whenever I can. The people are so friendly and always have a few nice words.'

Gordon Hodgson

Date of birth: 13 October 1952, Newcastle upon Tyne
Died: April 1999

Mansfield Town record:

Appearances: League 184, FA Cup 15, League Cup 14
Goals: League 23, FA Cup 1, League Cup 0
Debut: 17 August 1974 v Southport (h) won 2–1

Also played for: Newcastle United, Oxford United, Peterborough United

IF A movie were ever made recreating the Stags' Fourth Division title success of 1974–75, then they could always ask Zinedine Zidane to play the role of Gordon Hodgson. Admittedly the French maestro would need time in make-up to acquire the necessary flowing blonde locks, sideburns and 'tache, but football-wise he would be perfect.

Alright, the comparison's a little extreme, but Hodgy made Mansfield Town tick. Like 'ZZ' he was the midfield link-man, the glue bonding everything together – he was a wonderfully gifted footballer and a top bloke.

A native of the north-east, he fulfilled the ambition of every Newcastle schoolboy by joining his home-town club. Graduating through the ranks he made a handful of appearances in the Magpies' first team and was a non-playing squad member of their 1974 FA Cup final side.

Just a few months later he signed for Mansfield Town, sparking off a period of immense satisfaction for the club's followers. Gordon had been the first signing made by new manager Dave Smith – the first piece in his jigsaw and one of the most important!

Apart from his mastery in the centre of the park, Gordon was to become a prolific goalscorer, netting 10 in the league in his first season, many of them from long-range. It was the Stags' number 10 who earned his supporters some major bragging rights when his winner gave the Fourth Division Champions a 1–0 victory over League Champions Derby County, in a specially arranged end-of-the-season match. Mansfield Town – unofficially the best side in the land!

Unsurprisingly, Gordon was included in the PFA's Fourth Division Team of the Year, along with teammates Sandy Pate and Ray Clarke. Gordon was tagged 'Mr Consistency'. They might as well have called him 'Mr Fitness'. He only missed two matches during his four years with Mansfield, both through suspension.

During the Division Three title-winning run Gordon was appointed to succeed Pate as club captain and it was he who proudly collected the trophy.

A transfer fee of £35,000 took Gordon from Field Mill to Oxford United in September 1978. The move came as something of a surprise to the player but he took time to thank the fans who had been so supportive of him and his family. Later he played for Peterborough United before retiring from the game to join the Police Force.

Gordon Hodgson died in April 1999, aged just 46.

Paul Holland

Date of birth: 8 July 1973, Lincoln

Mansfield Town record:

Appearances: League 156, FA Cup 7, League Cup 11, Others 9
Goals: League 25, FA Cup 3, League Cup 0, Others 1
Debut: 11 May 1991 v Crewe Alexandra (a) lost 0–3

Also played for: Sheffield United, Chesterfield

IF PAUL Holland had been seaside rock, he would have Mansfield Town running right through his middle! Rarely has such a player worn the Stags shirt with so much pride. Puffing out his chest, you knew he'd die for the cause. Even after a stint playing for 'the old enemy across the border', he was welcomed back at Field Mill in a coaching capacity.

Paul had emerged through the youth team ranks to make his Stags debut while still just 17. A box-to-box runner with limitless energy, he immediately looked at ease despite his tender years.

He made 38 league appearances for the Stags in 1991–92, his first full season in the game. It was probably no coincidence that his emergence occurred in a successful promotion-winning campaign.

Never short of confidence, Paul was guaranteed to enjoy cult status after collecting his first goal for the club, away at Chesterfield. He scored five more that season but it was his all-round game that caught the eye. Passing, tackling, shooting – it all came naturally for the youngster they called 'Dutch'.

In full flight, he shared similarities with Paul Gascoigne. Some would say there was only ever one Gazza – Stags fans would say there was only ever one Paul Holland! The former Sleaford schoolboy racked up the appearances and the accolades and it was clear that Mansfield Town had a hot property on their books.

Sizeable bids were allegedly rejected before his eventual departure in the summer of 1995. Before he left, he helped the Stags into the play-offs, scoring his final goal for the club just as he'd scored the first – away at Chesterfield.

Paul's peers had voted him into the PFA Third Division side that season and he'd earned England Under-21 recognition, to go with the schoolboy caps he'd won several years earlier. While in Toulon, representing his country in the prestigious end-of-season tournament, Dave Bassett had flown out to sign him for Sheffield United for £250,000, plus certain clauses relating to the number of appearances he would make.

Alas, upon leaving Mansfield, Paul's career was continually interrupted by injuries and he only made 18 appearances for the Blades before joining Chesterfield. Cruelly he was forced to retire early, ending a career that had promised so much. Stags boss Stuart Watkiss invited Paul to return to Field Mill to coach the youngsters. It was an opportunity that he couldn't refuse.

His infectious enthusiasm and love of the game has ensured that another generation of talented juniors have graduated through into the first team.

To gauge the esteem in which Paul is still held you only have to hear the fans when a young midfielder makes his first start in the game. 'I wonder if he'll be the new Paul Holland?' they ask. There can be no greater compliment to Paul than that.

Ivan Hollett

Date of birth: 22 April 1940, Pinxton, Derbyshire

Mansfield Town record:

Appearances: League 98, FA Cup 3, League Cup 6
Goals: League 40, FA Cup 5, League Cup 2
Debut: 4 October 1958 v QPR (h) lost 3–4

Also played for: Derby County, Sutton Town, Chesterfield, Crewe Alexandra, Cambridge United, Hereford United

DURING a successful playing career Ivan Hollett hit three hat-tricks for the Stags' senior team. Forty years later he was still doing his bit for Mansfield Town, coaching youngsters and sharing his love of the game.

His first club was Derby County, with whom he played as an amateur but, after impressing while at Sutton Town, he joined Mansfield Town shortly after his 18th birthday.

He only played twice in his first season on the staff but made more of an impact the following term with 15 league goals in just 21 appearances, including three at Field Mill in a 4–1 win over Accrington Stanley. His tally, in 1959–60, matched that of Arthur Fitzsimmons as joint leading scorer.

Another hat-trick arrived in November 1960 at home against Barrow and he hit a third in the promotion season of 1962–63, although that one came in the FA Cup against Hounslow.

Ivan played under three managers at Mansfield: Sam Weaver, Raich Carter and Tommy Cummings. Just short of his 100th league match for the club Ivan was allowed to move to Chesterfield in circumstances which would seem quite bizarre today. The Saltergate club were rocked when a serious motor accident deprived them of four players. Ralph Hunt died and teammates Ron Powell, Doug Wragg and Peter Stringfellow sustained career-ending injuries. In the most neighbourly of gestures, the Stags allowed Ivan to join the Spireites to help compensate for their sad loss.

Over the next four seasons he scored 65 goals in just over 150 appearances for Chesterfield. A move to the First Division, with Stoke City, was later agreed, but Ivan sustained a serious injury before the deal was completed and the transfer was called off.

Later in his career he completed an unusual 'double' by playing for both Cambridge United and then Hereford United during their respective first seasons in the Football League.

After his playing career had ended Ivan returned to the Mansfield area and joined the mining engineering industry. His passion for the game, and extensive knowledge, hasn't been wasted. Since the early 1980's Ivan has given up many thousands of spare hours to help coach some of the club's brightest young schoolboy stars.

Dave Hollins

Date of birth: 4 February 1938, Bangor, North Wales

Mansfield Town record:

Appearances: League 111, FA Cup 12, League Cup 3
Debut: 25 February 1967 v Oxford United (a) lost 1–2

Also played for: Brighton and Hove Albion, Newcastle United, Nottingham Forest, Aldershot, Portsmouth, Romford

IT WAS a question that every Mansfield schoolboy of the time knew the answer to. 'Name the pair of brothers, one of whom plays for Wales while the other plays for England.'

While Guildford-born brother John, a battling midfielder with Chelsea, had won a cap for England in 1967, Dave Hollins had represented Wales 11 times, including a couple of games against Brazil, the reigning World Champions, and a match against England at Wembley. Apart from the question of the brothers' nationality, there was also the positional side of their game: Dave was a goalie!

Sadly for the Field Mill faithful, although he probably didn't know it at the time, Dave Hollins's international career had already ended by the time he joined the Stags for £2,500 from Newcastle United in February 1967. Dave had begun his career with Brighton and Hove Albion, joining the staff in 1955 and making 66 appearances for them. In March 1960 he was transferred to Newcastle United for £11,000 and he made an instant impression, saving a penalty against Spurs on his debut.

He'd already played for his national Under-23 side and won the first of those senior Welsh caps, as a substitute in Brazil in May 1962, before starting against Mexico a week later. By the time Dave moved to Mansfield, he had accumulated a wealth of experience, playing 121 times for Newcastle United.

Alan Cummings signed Dave to replace Alan Humphries as first choice 'keeper but it was under new manager Tommy Eggleston that the goalkeeper played his part in the most glorious season the club has experienced. The 1968–69 FA Cup giant-killing side will forever be remembered and it was Dave who kept a clean sheet against West Ham United in that remarkable 3–0 encounter.

Well as he played in that game, he was outstanding in the sixth round tie against Leicester City. With the nation watching, as the featured game on *Match of the Day*, Dave Hollins was breathtakingly brilliant. He had no chance with Rodney Fern's winner for the visitors but he pulled off save after save to keep his side in the contest.

At just under six feet in height, Dave was a good shot-stopper and commanded his area well. It was a much easier game for the Stags central defenders when 'the Welshman' was in goal!

During the following season, Graham Brown began to get more and more opportunities in the Stags goal, and Dave was loaned out to Nottingham Forest for a while – youngster Duncan McKenzie coming the other way to gain a taste of league football at Field Mill. Hollins made nine appearances during his stint at the City Ground.

At the end of the 1969–70 season Dave Hollins was given a free transfer to Aldershot. He spent just one season there, which also included a month on loan at Portsmouth, before going into the non-league game with Romford.

Simon Ireland

Date of birth: 23 November 1971, Barnstaple, Devon

Mansfield Town record:

Appearances: League 93, FA Cup 7, League Cup 9, Others 3
Goals: League 13, FA Cup 1, League Cup 1, Others 0
Debut: 19 March 1994 v Preston North End (a) lost 1–3

Also played for: Huddersfield Town, Wrexham, Blackburn Rovers, Doncaster Rovers

SOME Stags fans will recall Simon Ireland for his speedy runs down the right flank, while others will reflect that he was one of the first converts of the trend towards wearing cycling shorts under the traditional kit.

In reality though, Simon Ireland earns his rightful place as a Mansfield Town legend for scoring the winning goal against Leeds United, in a League Cup tie at Elland Road, in September 1994.

Although the tie was played over two legs, the only goal came early in the first meeting. Reporter Simon Mapletoft described the historic winning header in his match report in the *Chad*. 'The only breakthrough of the game came after 17 minutes. Kevin Noteman's corner was headed down by Holland into the path of the unmarked Stewart Hadley, who aimed another header at the far post. Ireland seized upon the opportunity and flung himself at the ball to send over 1,000 travelling Stags fans into a frenzy.'

Brought up in the Halifax area, Simon began his professional career at another Yorkshire club, Huddersfield Town. He'd made just 10 league starts for the Terriers, and spent a short spell on loan at Wrexham, before Kenny Dalglish stepped in with a bid of £200,000 to sign Simon for Blackburn Rovers.

Seen as a potential understudy to Stuart Ripley, Rovers' outstanding right-winger, Simon had to bide his time at Ewood Park. He made one substitute appearance for the first team, at Manchester City, but then broke an ankle and was sidelined for a season.

Stags boss Andy King took him to Field Mill, initially on loan, once his fitness had been confirmed. The signing was later made permanent for a fee of around £25,000, with sell-on clauses.

Apart from his goal at Elland Road, Simon also scored another Cup goal for the Stags, although this time the outcome wasn't as memorable. An FA Cup tie at Field Mill in January 1995 saw the home side fly into a 2–0 lead after just 10 minutes. The second goal was scored by Ireland, although there was an element of good fortune as his cross sailed straight over the stranded 'keeper and into the net. A second-half response from the Division One side turned the deficit into a 3–2 victory.

After making just over a century of appearances for Mansfield Town, Simon Ireland was allowed to move to Doncaster Rovers in the autumn of 1997. He later moved into non-league football with Boreham Wood but he will forever be linked to 'that night at Elland Road!'

Harry Johnson

Date of birth: 4 January 1899, Ecclesfield, Sheffield
Died: May 1981

Mansfield Town record:

Appearances: League 163, FA Cup 7
Goals: League 104, FA Cup 8
Debut: 29 August 1931 v Swindon Town (h) won 3–2

Also played for: Sheffield United

NO ONE has scored more league goals for Mansfield Town than Harry Johnson and no one has scored more league goals for Sheffield United than Harry Johnson! This is a simple enough sentence, illustrating how influential a player he was at two different football clubs.

A native of Sheffield, he joined the Blades at 17 years of age but then had to join the Army and fight at the Battle of Verdun in World War One. Post-war, he returned to Bramall Lane and set about scoring goals with stunning frequency. Over a 12-year period, he scored a total of 205 goals for United. His best seasons were 1927–28 and 1928–29, when he scored 33 goals in each. He had won an FA Cup winners' medal in 1925 when he played in the Blades 1–0 win over Cardiff City, at Wembley.

From fine footballing stock, the Johnsons are fairly unique in FA Cup history. Harry's father, Harry Senior, had won FA Cup winners' medals with Sheffield United in both 1899 and 1902 and brother Tom appeared for the same club when they lost in the 1936 final, to Arsenal.

Most observers feel that Harry Johnson was particularly unfortunate not to win any England caps. He did make an appearance for the Football League XI and scored a hat-trick in a 9–1 win. Everton's Dixie Dean took the plaudits, though, by grabbing four!

In July 1931 Johnson ended his association with the Sheffield club by joining the Stags. He made his debut in the club's first Football League fixture and netted a total of 32 goals that season. That tally made him top scorer, as he was for the club's first four seasons in the league.

Harry liked to score goals – and he liked to get them in clusters. He netted the first three hat-tricks for Mansfield Town in the Football League, against Luton Town, New Brighton and Darlington – all at Field Mill.

Astonishingly, Harry remained a part-time player throughout his career and on retiring from the game he continued working as an analytical chemist at Hadfields Steelworks in Sheffield.

He finally retired in 1963 and died in May 1981, aged 82.

Dai Jones

Date of birth: 31 March 1941, Ton Pentre, Rhondda

Mansfield Town record:

Appearances: League 130, FA Cup 7, League Cup 3
Goals: League 32, FA Cup 2, League Cup 0
Debut: 23 December 1967 v Scunthorpe United (h) won 3–0

Also played for: Millwall, Newport County

SIGNED by Tommy Eggleston for £1,500, from Newport County, Dai Jones couldn't have made a bigger initial impact at Mansfield Town. He scored in each of his first four matches for the club, all won.

David Albert Brynmawr Jones had begun his footballing career with his local Welsh side, Ton Pentre, and had been good enough to gain Welsh youth international caps.

Millwall's early interest resulted in Dai spending a season at the Den, although a switch to Newport County ignited his career. Two successful seasons at Somerton Park saw him reap 25 goals from 82 outings and brought a move to Field Mill.

Partnering Bob Ledger in the Stags attack, Jones had a festive season to remember, scoring on the 23, 26 and 30 December, and again, after a series of postponements, when the club played their next match three weeks later. What a Christmas present for the fans! Understandably, the 'Welsh poacher' wasn't able to continue scoring in the same prolific vein but he ended his first part-season at the Mill as top scorer with eight goals.

Injury disrupted his progress the following term, meaning a frustrating time on the sidelines while the club were writing their FA Cup giant-killing headlines. 'Jonesy' had a cup story to tell of his own, the year after, when he netted both Mansfield goals in a 2–0 win at Bloomfield Road, against Blackpool.

The Seasiders had humbled mighty Arsenal in the previous round but, as the *Chad* reported, it was the visitors who gained an early advantage: 'Twice in a minute the darting Dai Jones was hustled off the ball and a corner conceded as Town tore into the attack. And there was not a defender within four yards when Jones nipped in to head Jimmy Goodfellow's third corner kick into the net to put Stags in front after just four minutes'. Jones's second came in the final minute when he latched onto a through ball from skipper John Quigley, to set up a fifth round FA Cup tie at Elland Road, against Leeds United.

The match at Leeds and a League Cup tie at Anfield, against Liverpool, were probably the biggest matches Dai would play for the club, although his final goal for Mansfield Town was scored on another of English football's most illustrious stages when the Stags beat Aston Villa 1–0 at Villa Park in September 1971.

That would have been a fitting postscript to a relatively successful Field Mill career, but Dai's last match for the club was a local derby defeat at Meadow Lane, against Notts County. Manager Jock Basford was sacked after the game and Dai accepted an offer to return home to play for his former club, Newport County.

Mark Kearney

Date of birth: 12 June 1962, Ormskirk, Lancashire

Mansfield Town record:

Appearances: League 250, FA Cup 12, League Cup 18, Others 22
Goals: League 29, FA Cup 1, League Cup 2, Others 4
Debut: 19 March 1983 v Colchester United (h) drew 1–1

Also played for: Everton, Bury

MARK Kearney was one of the Stags' Wembley heroes and an integral part of the club for nine seasons. Ian Greaves signed him from Everton in 1983, and the two have remained friends, and in touch, ever since. 'He was quite simply the best manager I have ever worked for. He was respected by everyone who met him', says Mark.

The Freight Rover triumph was undoubtedly the highlight of Mark's stay at Mansfield and he says the whole campaign was enjoyable. 'I just think we knew all along that we were going to win. The team spirit was unbelievable and that saw us through some really difficult matches.'

It was Mark's nerveless penalty that clinched the victory at Ayresome Park over Middlesbrough, the heavy favourites for the trophy, and after a nail-biting semi-final win over Chester it was on to Wembley. 'We just ran the whole range of emotions that day. At times we looked like we were going to win, then we appeared out of it, but Hitchy made some wonderful saves in the shoot-out and we got there!'

As the regular penalty taker, it had been Mark's responsibility to step up that day to take the Stags' first spot-kick in the shadow of Wembley's famous twin towers. 'I wasn't too sure about what I was going to do as I'd scored a penalty against Bristol City just a couple of weeks earlier. Anyway, I decided to hit it for the other corner this time and was pleased to see the 'keeper go the wrong way!'

Success at Wembley doesn't deserve to be forgotten – and isn't in the Kearney household. 'I get the medal out quite often. As a prize itself, it doesn't look much but it brings back so many happy memories.'

Mark enjoyed a spell as skipper of the club and starred in a successful promotion campaign but above all else it's the way he was treated at Field Mill that delights him the most. 'Stags fans are just fantastic. I've nothing but praise for the way they treated me and for the atmosphere they created during my time at the club.'

That support was particularly appreciated when he broke a leg against Fulham in September 1987, effectively writing off his season. He returned for the next campaign, usually at left-back, although occasionally in midfield, and totted up 250 league appearances before moving on to Bury.

Nicknamed 'Scouse', he had a stint as player-coach at Telford under former Stags boss George Foster and has worked at both Shrewsbury and Northampton, apart from a two-year spell back at Field Mill as coach.

In recent times Mark Kearney has been a welcome visitor to the Field Mill press box as a working member of the media and will take up a coaching appointment with the Derby County Academy for the 2004–05 season. His support for Mansfield Town has never wavered and in May 2004 he journeyed to the Millennium Stadium, as a fan, to see the Yellows on their big day out.

Ray Keeley

Date of birth: 25 December 1946, Battersea, London

Mansfield Town record:

Appearances: League 52, FA Cup 11, League Cup 2
Goals: League 5, FA Cup 5, League Cup 1
Debut: 10 August 1968 v Brighton & Hove Albion (a) won 2–1

Also played for: Charlton Athletic, Exeter City, Crawley Town, Poole Town

SOMEWHAT ironically, for a lad born in London, Ray Keeley's moment of destiny occurred against a side from the capital. Ray only played 65 times in the Mansfield Town first team, but whenever anyone mentions 'that night, that win' the memories of his stunning goal come flooding back.

Mighty West Ham United, with their trio of World Cup winners, turned up and were turned over. The FA Cup fifth round tie they thought would never happen eventually got under way after five postponements due to heavy snowfalls. The chances of a shock result intensified with a close range goal from Dudley Roberts. On 37 minutes it was time for the footballing gods to smile on Ray Keeley.

Among those in a packed Field Mill press box that evening was reporter Laurie Pignon. His match report, which appeared in the *Daily Sketch* newspaper the following morning, eloquently described the goal.

'The second by Ray Keeley was a complete and magnificent contrast. It was a 20-yard volley which he later described as "A dream goal which you never think will really happen until it does". I echo those sentiments! West Ham goalkeeper Bobby Ferguson had punched out a Goodfellow shot right on to Keeley's left boot. His timing was as accurate as a striking pin on a cannon.'

Reporter Laurie was clearly impressed but the young forward was dogged by injuries and was sidelined for much of the next season. He eventually left Field Mill in 1970 to join non-league Poole Town.

His playing career had begun at Charlton Athletic, but after making just one first-team appearance he was sold to Exeter City. He scored 10 goals in 45 appearances for the Grecians but his league career seemed at an end when he was allowed to move to Crawley Town.

Jock Basford was assistant manager to Tommy Eggleston at Mansfield and he'd coached Keeley at Charlton. Realising his potential, he persuaded the forward to move north.

Ray's time with the Stags might have been relatively brief but he did make an impact, especially in the FA Cup. Apart from his 'headline-making goal', he also scored against Tow Law Town and Rotherham United in the 1968–69 cup run and against Bury and Shrewsbury Town the following season when he also appeared, as a substitute, against Leeds United at Elland Road.

Kevin Kent

Date of birth: 19 March 1965, Stoke-on-Trent

Mansfield Town record:

Appearances: League 229, FA Cup 13, League Cup 10, Others 23
Goals: League 36, FA Cup 13, League Cup 2, Others 5
Debut: 18 September 1985 v Orient (h) drew 1–1

Also played for: West Bromwich Albion, Newport County, Port Vale

ON A sunny day in May 1987, Kevin Kent wrote his name into the history books of Mansfield Town. He became the first Stags player to score on the hallowed turf of Wembley Stadium. Indeed, Kevin reflects, 'Like every footballer it was always my dream to score at Wembley and on that day I was fortunate enough to achieve one of my ambitions. It was the icing on the cake, on what was a fantastic day.'

Kevin also tucked away his spot-kick that day, as the side emerged victorious from a penalty shoot-out but, understandably, his goal from open play is etched into his memory. 'Keith Cassells was racing down the left and I knew he wouldn't be able to put his cross towards the far post so I set off for the near post, and when I arrived, so did the ball – Cass didn't let me down!'

With his mop of dark, curly hair, Kevin's stature within the club's history was guaranteed from that moment on but, during his six seasons with Town, he did much, much more. Usually employed on the right-hand side of the midfield quartet, Kevin created far more goals than he ever scored himself but his unselfish vision, skill and imagination made him a big favourite with supporters and teammates alike. He only missed one match during his first two full seasons with the club and he weighed in with 17 league goals during that period.

Ironically, for a player later to join Port Vale, his best individual day in Town's colours came at Field Mill, against the Valiants. Just before Christmas 1987, Kevin scored all four goals against his future club, in a match played on a Sunday.

Kevin had played for both West Brom and Newport County before his arrival at Mansfield but it was at Field Mill that his career really took off. He will always be remembered with the deepest affection at Field Mill for providing a magical moment in the history of Mansfield Town Football Club and a moment that no Stags supporter, no matter what age, is likely ever to forget.

Kevin later enjoyed more success at Wembley, winning the Autoglass Trophy there with Vale in 1993. Since retiring from the game he has followed the fortunes of Port Vale, enhancing his reputation as one of the best radio summarisers around.

Tony Kenworthy

Date of birth: 31 October 1958, Leeds

Mansfield Town record:

Appearances: League 100, FA Cup 6, League Cup 5, Others 13
Goals: League 0, FA Cup 0, League Cup 0, Others 0
Debut: 14 March 1986 v Colchester United (a) drew 0–0

Also played for: Sheffield United

THERE can't be many sports-mad schoolboys that haven't dreamt of scoring the winning goal at Wembley. Every playground in the country has witnessed the same scenario being recreated countless times. Sadly, for so many of those youngsters, the dreams remain unfulfilled. But Tony Kenworthy's prayers – and those of all Stags fans – were answered beneath the twin towers of Wembley on 24 May 1987.

Penalty shoot-outs were still in their infancy then. Few had actually taken place, and there had certainly been none to decide the outcome of a major final. Over 120 minutes of draining, tense play, the players of Bristol City and Mansfield Town had locked horns and come out level.

After five kicks apiece in the shoot-out it was all square. Then Kevin Hitchcock, in the Stags goal, saved from David Moyes. A cool head was needed – and some steely nerve. Tony Kenworthy delivered both as he drove beyond Keith Waugh in the City goal. Mansfield had won!

The bulk of Tony's professional career had been spent at Sheffield United. He'd joined the Bramall Lane staff as an apprentice and turned full-time professional during July 1976. Over the next decade he made a total of 286 appearances and played in a couple of promotion-winning sides.

He joined Mansfield on loan at first, and was able to make an immediate impact. His experience was vital over the closing stages as Stags scraped into third place to secure promotion. During the subsequent close-season Tony's move to Field Mill was made permanent. Adding some composed reassurance to the Stags back-line Tony was a regular for the next couple of seasons.

He then began to suffer badly with injuries. During his time at Field Mill he was absent, at various times, with knee, ankle and finally Achilles tendon problems.

His final appearance for the club was his only one of the 1989–90 season – against Blackpool. Fittingly, it was his 100th league game for the club.

Usually playing at the heart of the defence, Tony occasionally filled in at left-back but in neither position did he get on the scoresheet for the Stags. So it is all the more remarkable that his decisive penalty at Wembley will remain in the record books forever.

Colin Larkin

Date of birth: 27 April 1982, Dundalk

Mansfield Town record (to end of season 2003–04):

Appearances: League 58, FA Cup 4, League Cup 0, Others 5
Goals: League 14, FA Cup 1, League Cup 0, Others 0
Debut: 10 August 2002 v Plymouth Argyle (h) won 4–3

Also played for: Wolverhampton Wanderers, Kidderminster Harriers

GIVEN time, Colin Larkin may well establish himself as one of the leading strikers in Mansfield Town's history. By his own admission, he has remained on the periphery of the first team during his first couple of seasons with the club. Nevertheless, he was responsible for the most spontaneous and joyous pitch invasion ever seen at Field Mill and then involved in one of the major talking points in Stags' recent history.

Colin's coolly-taken penalty kick decided a play-off semi-final shoot-out, against Northampton Town, in May 2004 and set the happy Yellows up for a big day out at the Millennium Stadium. 'I was just pleased to get the opportunity to take the winning kick' he says. 'Everyone else had done their job and Kev had made a fine save so it was just a matter of keeping a cool head and making sure I hit the target.'

The young Irishman certainly hit the target, sending Cobblers' goalkeeper Lee Harper the wrong way. Although the ensuing scenes of celebration were in recognition of an appearance on the big stage at Cardiff, they will also be remembered by those watching from behind the goal.

With advanced plans to move home supporters away from the North Stand, on police advice, it was perhaps fitting that the last act there for Stags fans to celebrate was a moment of pure theatre. 'I'd scored against Northampton in the league, just a couple of weeks earlier, and felt confident after going on. I didn't really expect it to come down to penalties, though.'

If the events of the semi-final weren't dramatic enough, there was more in store at the Millennium Stadium. Colin replaced Craig Disley after an hour of the game and made a huge impact. With 90 minutes up on the clock the Stags pressed forward. Tom Curtis crossed from the right, Laurent D'Jaffo headed back across the goal and Colin swept the ball into the back of the Huddersfield Town net. The thousands of fans bedecked in yellow rejoiced and Colin ran off to celebrate.

Sadly those celebrations were cut short with an assistant's flag ruling that the cross had drifted over the goal-line before Laurent's head-back. Any number of television replays couldn't confirm or deny the decision. Colin was denied the opportunity of taking a kick in yet another shoot-out, as it was all over before he had a turn.

A former Republic of Ireland Under-18 international, Colin joined the staff at Wolves and made his debut for them in August 1999, aged just 17. A season on loan at Kidderminster Harriers gave him invaluable first team experience and prompted a bid from Mansfield Town. His debut was memorable, with Colin scoring the decider in a seven-goal Field Mill thriller against Plymouth Argyle.

Niggling injuries hampered his progress but the striker quickly became a firm fans' favourite and 'Super Col' has time on his side in which to write himself into another chapter in the history of the club.

John Lathan

Date of birth: 12 April 1952, Sunderland

Mansfield Town record:

Appearances: League 103, FA Cup 8, League Cup 5
Goals: League 15, FA Cup 0, League Cup 1
Debut: 24 February 1974 v Newport County (h) won 2–1

Also played for: Sunderland, Carlisle United, Barnsley, Portsmouth

A SOLID rather than spectacular performer, John Lathan was a valued member of Dave Smith's Championship-winning midfield. Initally, he wasn't too keen on being used as a makeweight in the transfer from Mansfield of another player. Why would he? He was a Sunderland fan who, since turning professional in April 1969, had gone on to make over 50 first-team appearances for his favourite side.

The deal eventually went through with former Stag Dennis Longhorn moving to Roker Park, and John coming to Field Mill. Mansfield received £200,000 in cash as well – not the worst bit of business they've ever done! He made his debut in the same number seven shirt he was to wear for the next two years and made an immediate impact – scoring in a home win over Newport County.

Goals came with great regularity at first – he netted five in his first 12 games for the club – and this proved to be the most prolific spell of his career.

However, less than a month after John's arrival at Field Mill, the manager who had signed him, Danny Williams, had departed. Having just settled into his new routine John now had to convince a new boss of his worth to the team.

Lathan's immediate problem was that he had a suspension hanging over him and so he missed the opening two games of the 1974–75 season, at home to Southport in the league and away at Doncaster Rovers in the League Cup. But John needn't have worried – he soon became a key component in Dave Smith's assault on the title and the first two games would turn out to be the only matches he was absent from throughout the whole campaign.

Standing just 5ft 7in tall in his bare feet, John became a tenacious tackler and an essential supply line to the front two. With McCaffrey causing mayhem on the other flank, Lathan helped supply the ammunition from the right.

Overall that 1974–75 season was an outstanding success – both for the team and for John Lathan individually. His nine league goals had been a major contribution and he deservedly pocketed his medal.

During the early part of the following season John suffered a broken collarbone during a match at Bury. That put him out for several months but, upon regaining his place in the side, Mansfield accepted a bid of £11,000 from Carlisle United and sold him.

Three and a half years later, after a loan spell at Barnsley and a move to Portsmouth, John moved back to Field Mill, for a season under Mick Jones. It wasn't the happiest of times and, having played in the side that gained promotion from Division Four, John was now a part of the side that had been relegated once more.

John received training in the treatment of sports injuries and, after retiring from the game altogether, began a new career in that profession.

Mick Laverick

Date of birth: 13 March 1954, Trimdon, County Durham

Mansfield Town record:

Appearances: League 89, FA Cup 5, League Cup 9
Goals: League 13, FA Cup 1, League Cup 4
Debut: 12 August 1972 v Northampton Town (h) won 1–0

Also played for: Southend United, Huddersfield Town, York City, Boston United

MICK Laverick is still waiting for his Championship medal! Thirty years after Dave Smith's side won the Division Four title, Mick was still medal-less. 'I had an injury hit season and only made 11 league appearances. I've always heard people at other clubs saying they'd qualified for medals after playing 10 games but I didn't get one!' There would have been no debate about it, had Mick not sustained a cartilage injury mid-season. 'I did it playing for the reserves, against Chesterfield, and missed about three months.'

A regular in the Stags first team, both before and after his injury, Mick did, at least, have the satisfaction of picking up another medal, on his Stags debut. 'My first outing for the senior side was in the Notts FA County Cup Cup Final in May 1972' he says. 'We beat Notts County 3–1 at home.'

That summer was spent preparing for his first season in league football and the youngster was in Danny Williams's side for the opening match of the new campaign. His first goal came at Field Mill, in a League Cup tie, on 16 August 1972 against Lincoln City.

Mick's family had moved down to Ollerton, from the north-east, when he was a youngster and he'd impressed in local league football. His breakthrough seemed to come when he was invited to Huddersfield for a week-long trial. The Terriers, however, bossed by Ian Greaves at the time, decided not to pursue their interest. Shortly afterwards Jock Basford saw him play and invited him to Field Mill for a trial. He was soon taken on and spent five seasons at the club.

A leggy midfielder, Mick scored some crucial goals for the Stags, with well-timed bursts into the box. 'My two favourite goals for the club would have to be against Wrexham and Crystal Palace. The Wrexham one was a diving header from Ray Clarke's cross, in an FA Cup replay staged at Villa Park. The Palace goal was just a volley banged from 25 yards into the net at the Quarry Lane End.'

The arrival of Peter Morris as the Stags' player-manager reduced the midfield options and Mick decided it was time to move on. 'Peter played me up front a couple of times but I was happy when Dave Smith came in and took me to Southend with him.'

Mick's career ended as it had started – with a medal. 'I'd ended up at Boston United and was having trouble with arthritis in my left hip. I decided to call it a day but agreed to help out for an FA Trophy quarter-final. We won – and then won the semi – to reach the final. On the day we lost to Wealdstone, with Vinnie Jones in their squad, and I thought to end my career by playing at Wembley Stadium was the perfect way to finish.'

After retiring from the game Mick joined the Prison Service and has been employed at HMP Ranby for several years.

Liam Lawrence

Date of birth: 14 December 1981, Retford, Notts

Mansfield Town record:

Appearances: League 136, FA Cup 8, League Cup 3, Others 6
Goals: League 35, FA Cup 5, League Cup 0, Others 0
Debut: 11 January 2000 v Blackpool (h) lost 0–1

MOST observers feel that Liam Lawrence is destined to reach the very top of his chosen profession. Supremely gifted, and with a determination to match, he has established himself as the leading light among the Stags' recent crop of home-grown talent.

Out of contract at the end of the 2003–04 season, few Mansfield fans begrudged Liam the opportunity of leaving Field Mill to further his career at a higher level with Sunderland. The only disappointment for the youngster was that his final game for the club, in May 2004, ended on such a low.

'To lose the play-off final on penalties was just heart-breaking', he says. 'I was on the grass at the end. The Huddersfield players were celebrating all around me, yet I could look into the stand and see my family and friends still sat there. I just felt that we'd let everyone down.'

The emotion of the defeat would have been hard for all the Stags players to bear but no one could truly feel let-down. An end-of-season trip to Cardiff had been made possible by a rollercoaster campaign with Liam at the forefront of most of the sides' best moments.

After being attached to Nottingham Forest's youngsters from the age of nine, Liam suffered the disappointment of being rejected at just 14. He still recalls the despondency and the way his family responded. 'My dad, Shaun, was terrific. He has been the single biggest influence on my career. Not just for driving me about for training and games but also for having the confidence in me.'

Forest's loss was clearly Mansfield's gain and he soon made a big impression after being taken on at Field Mill. His development was rapid and he made two league appearances at the end of the 1999–00 season, after a debut appearance as substitute in the Auto Windscreen Shield competition.

After cementing his first-team spot he quickly became a firm favourite, turning in a series of stunning, eye-catching performances. Liam himself is quick to assess his own game: 'I feel I'm comfortable on the ball and always capable of making things happen.'

Usually starting on the right-hand side of midfield, Liam has been known to venture in-field to create openings. His own determination to do well is evident. 'I'm naturally competitive', he says. 'I just want to do well all of the time!'

Apart from the consistency of his performances, Liam will inevitably be linked with his penalty-taking during his time at Field Mill. He successfully converted 12 during the 2003–04 season, often at crucial times. 'I practice them every day in training' he says. 'The more you practice the more confident you become!'

An FA Cup hat-trick against Wycombe, the first of his career, featured two spot-kicks and is high among his Field Mill memories. His favourite Stags goal, though, will be shared by many. 'The winner at Chesterfield in January 2003 has to be my most treasured moment for Mansfield. Four minutes into injury time – Jamie Clarke's free-kick, Rhys Day headed it on and I nodded it in. Then, mayhem – it was just brilliant!'

Tony Lowery

Date of birth: 6 July 1961, Wallsend, Northumberland

Mansfield Town record:

Appearances: League 252, FA Cup 15, League Cup 22, Others 26
Goals: League 19, FA Cup 2, League Cup 1, Others 5
Debut: 7 May 1983 v Peterborough United (a) lost 2–3

Also played for: West Bromwich Albion, Walsall, Carlisle United, Gateshead

CERTAIN players become unlikely crowd favourites – they are consistent rather than spectacular – but their commitment and will to win is beyond reproach. Tony Lowery was one such player.

Lowery first arrived at Field Mill on loan from West Bromwich Albion in April 1983, and just a month later the deal became permanent. He missed just one game during his first full season with Town. Adding some tactical nouse and competitive steel to the centre of the park, he chipped in with half a dozen goals. Tony simplified football – work hard and pass accurately seemed to be his motto!

Rarely absent from the starting line-up, he was a consistent performer in the side which was able to celebrate promotion after finishing third in Division Three in 1985–86. The following year he became one of the Stags' Wembley heroes, celebrating Freight Rover success over Bristol City. Along the route to the twin towers Tony had scored a vital goal away at Bury to set up a 2–1 win.

On the big day itself no one tried harder to wrest the initiative away from the City midfielders. After a lung-busting display he somehow still had the energy to race triumphantly upfield to be among the first to congratulate and celebrate with the winning penalty hero, Tony Kenworthy.

Aside from the Wembley triumph, Ian Greaves's side consolidated their league position, with a creditable 10th-place finish in the table. The 1987–88 campaign didn't go as well. Struggling for most of the year, the club did well to preserve its status in the Third Division. Lowery, consistent as ever, clocked up a fifth consecutive season in Mansfield yellow in which he'd played in 40 or more league matches.

Injuries then began to take their toll and, for long periods, George Foster had to make do without one of the most experienced players on his staff. In September 1990 the decision was made to loan Tony out to Walsall and the following summer he left the club permanently, with a move to Carlisle United.

He made just seven league appearances for the Cumbrians before moving into the non-league game in his native north-east. Initially he joined Gateshead, before becoming assistant manager at Blyth Spartans.

Having stamped his pedigree on that level Tony has, for many years, enjoyed a long and successful stint at Northern Premier League side Bedlington Terriers, where he holds the position of joint manager alongside Keith Perry.

Paul Matthews

Date of birth: 30 September 1946, Leicester

Mansfield Town record:

Appearances: League 124, FA Cup 11, League Cup 5
Goals: League 6, FA Cup 1, League Cup 0
Debut: 9 December 1972 v Workington (a) lost 0–2

Also played for: Leicester City, Southend United, Rotherham United, Northampton Town,
                 Heanor Town, Oadby Town

PAUL Matthews was one of the unsung heroes of the 1974–75 Championship-winning side. His role was simple – win the ball and give it to a teammate – and he fulfilled it with simple efficiency, playing in 44 of the 46 league games that season.

He'd begun his career at his home-town club, Leicester City, turning professional at the age of 18. Remarkably, he'd never played football until the age of 15, after attending a rugby-playing grammar school. Paul had excelled at the oval ball game, representing Leicestershire schools as a fly-half.

Football took precedence and he made 56 league appearances for the Filbert Street club, scoring five times. He collected a Division Two Championship medal in the 1970–71 season. After a short loan spell with Southend United, Paul joined Mansfield Town in December 1972, for a fee of £5,000.

He'd been used predominantly as a winger with the Foxes but under manager Danny Williams and then Dave Smith he was employed in a central midfield role.

Season 1973–74 was one to forget for Paul. Injured against Scunthorpe United in a pre-season friendly, he had to undergo surgery on a cartilage injury and was ruled out until Christmas. Not long after his return, Dave Smith took over as manager and Paul, fully fit again, really came to prominence. Protecting the back four, he allowed the gifted Gordon Hodgson to enjoy a free role in the centre of the park. Paul was always likely to join the attack himself and packed a powerful shot. He chipped in with several important strikes in a Stags shirt.

Apart from his league successes, Paul Matthews played in the march to the fifth round of the FA Cup in 1974–75 and in other big matches, against Coventry City, Wolves and Manchester City in the league cup, the following season.

The arrival of Peter Morris at Field Mill as player-manager limited Paul's opportunities but he still made 18 league appearances in the Division Three Championship-winning side, to complete the unusual achievement of collecting Division Two, Three and Four title medals, all in the space of six years.

In 1977 Paul moved to Rotherham United and later had a loan spell at Northampton Town, before moving into non-league football at both Heanor Town and Oadby Town. Paul remained in the game, scouting for Leicester City and coaching local youngsters in his native Leicestershire.

Jim McCaffrey

Date of birth: 12 October 1951, Luton, Bedfordshire

Mansfield Town record:

Appearances: League 178, FA Cup 15, League Cup 11
Goals: League 21, FA Cup 3, League Cup 3
Debut: 12 August 1972 v Northampton Town (h) won 1–0

Also played for: Nottingham Forest, Huddersfield Town, Portsmouth, Northampton Town

UNDOUBTEDLY Jim McCaffrey was one of the most exciting players ever to represent the Stags. Like most wide players, he would occasionally 'disappear' from matches but, on his day, he had the capacity to terrorise defences and lift the fans from their seats.

He began his footballing career with the St Albans Boys' Club, but was offered a trial by Leeds United. The Elland Road club failed to spot his potential but Nottingham Forest did, and he joined the City Ground staff.

Earlier he'd played for the England youth side, playing in the 'Little World Cup' alongside the likes of Steve Perryman and Steve Whitworth. He made a handful of appearances for the Forest first team but his chances were limited and in July 1972 he was signed, on a free transfer, by Mansfield Town boss Danny Williams.

Over the next four seasons he was rarely absent. He had sufficient pace to take him away from the fleetest of right backs and his all-round game improved considerably. Crosses were usually delivered with pinpoint accuracy and he had the ability to convert scoring opportunities when he ventured infield, away from the sanctuary of the left flank.

His goals output was good. Invariably his contributions would come at vital moments, clinching games as often as not. It was his winner at Bury that took the side into the fifth round of the FA Cup in 1975.

Jimmy McCaffrey, though, had the ability to do the unpredictable. He put 'bums on seats' – fans turned up just to see him and he usually sent them home happy, especially during the Division Four title-winning season of 1974–75. No wonder they called him 'the wizard of the wing!'

All great things come to an end and, although Jimmy played in enough games to qualify for a second Championship medal in the 1976–77 season, he was often overlooked by manager Peter Morris, with Johnny Miller being preferred on the wing.

He was transferred to Huddersfield Town and later played for Portsmouth and Northampton Town. After retiring in 1979 he became a newsagent in the Lake District, before taking up a similar position in Leicestershire.

An all-too-infrequent visitor to Field Mill nowadays, Jimmy McCaffrey is one of the real 'stars' to have represented the club.

John McClelland

Date of birth: 7 December 1955, Belfast

Mansfield Town record:

Appearances: League 125, FA Cup 8, League Cup 9
Goals: League 8, FA Cup 1, League Cup 2
Debut: 12 August 1978 v Darlington (h) lost 0–1

Also played for: Portadown, Cardiff City, Bangor City, Glasgow Rangers, Watford, Leeds United, Notts County, St Johnstone, Carrick Rangers, Wycombe Wanderers, Yeovil Town, Woking, Arbroath, Doncaster Rovers, Scunthorpe United, Darlington, Northern Ireland (53 caps)

Managed: St Johnstone

THEY say it's not what you know but who you know – and John McClelland may feel that certainly applies to him. In 1980 he was called into the Northern Ireland squad, becoming the first Mansfield Town player to receive a full international call-up. The manager of his home country, at the time, was Billy Bingham – the same manager who'd signed John for the Stags!

In the fullest of careers, the Belfast-born central-defender achieved the rare distinction of playing at the highest level in all four countries of the United Kingdom.

John had been a striker in the early days and chanced his arm with a move from Portadown to Cardiff City. Things didn't work out particularly well at Ninian Park and he was allowed to join non-league Bangor City after making just one first-team appearance.

Converted to a defender, he was brought to Field Mill by Bingham in May 1978. Although raw, John certainly showed promise. However, few observers would have predicted that such a successful career would follow.

The improvement in John's game was considerable and he became the backbone of the Stags' defence. He was an ever-present under Mick Jones in the 1980–81 season – as well as establishing himself in the Northern Ireland side.

For the record, while still a Stags player, John appeared in six international matches, playing against Scotland (twice), Sweden and in all three matches on a summer tour of Australia.

In May 1981 Glasgow Rangers stepped in with a bid of £90,000 to take him to Ibrox. Although it was a departure that the fans had dreaded, it had become increasingly apparent that a move was imminent.

John became the captain of his country and played at both the 1982 and 1986 World Cup Finals. Returning to English football, he played for Watford, and then Leeds United, where he won a league title in 1992. He then began to move around clubs with great regularity, incorporating his skill as a player with a first taste of management at St Johnstone.

Like a restless puppy he moved hither and thither between clubs until joining Darlington in 1996. On his debut for the club, against local rivals Hartlepool United, he had the misfortune to break a leg.

John finally accepted that he had to call time on a playing career that had taken him to the very top of his profession. Along the way, he had written himself into the Mansfield Town record books.

Ian McDonald

Date of birth: 10 May 1953, Barrow in Furness

Mansfield Town record:

Appearances: League 56, FA Cup 6, League Cup 6
Goals: League 4, FA Cup 1, League Cup 3
Debut: 16 August 1975 v Shrewsbury Town (h) lost 1–2

Also played for: Barrow, Workington, Liverpool, Colchester United, York City, Aldershot,
Farnborough Town

GOOD pro that he was, Ian McDonald can't lay any sort of claim to being the best midfielder Mansfield Town have ever had on their books but he did have his moment of glory.

His career had begun with his home-town club, Barrow, and he was the only professional left on the books when they were voted out of the league in 1972. He moved to local rivals Workington and his career began to flourish – to the extent that Bill Shankly, no less, signed him for Liverpool.

A debut goal for the Reds' reserves seemed to hail the arrival of a future star but he broke his foot in the same game and was effectively out of action for a year. Loan spells and irregular comebacks failed to rediscover the early promise and the Anfield Road club accepted an offer for his signature from Dave Smith, the Mansfield Town boss. He was with the Stags for barely more than a couple of years, yet the night of 12 November 1975 belonged to 'Super-Mac'.

Enhancing their reputation as cup giant-killers, the Yellows knocked First Division Wolves out of the League Cup at Field Mill, with McDonald scoring the only goal. The *Chad* match report made much of the fact that Mansfield Town would now play Manchester City in round five, describing the winning strike in economical terms. 'To Ian McDonald goes the credit for scoring the 37th-minute goal, which took the Stags through, from an opening set up by Gordon Hodgson following a Sandy Pate throw-in.'

McDonald's right-foot drive beyond Gary Pierce, in the Wolves goal, was the highlight of his stay at the club, although even greater things had been forecast when he had first joined the club for a fee of £10,000. Ian's debut in the Stags' colours was in the pre-season Anglo-Scottish Cup competition but his league bow ended in defeat, despite a goalscoring debut, against Shrewsbury Town.

His brief stay at Field Mill ended in November 1977, when he was allowed to move on to York City. At last, he found some consistency in his game and made over 200 appearances for the Minstermen. His final league club was Aldershot, whom he captained and later managed.

Duncan McKenzie

Date of birth: 10 June 1950, Grimsby

Mansfield Town record:

Appearances: League 16
Goals: League 10
Debut: 9 March 1970 v Barnsley (h) won 2–0

Also played for: Nottingham Forest, Leeds United, Anderlecht (Belgium), Everton, Chelsea,
Blackburn Rovers

IT probably says more about the selection policy of our national team than about the player's talents, but the fact is that Duncan McKenzie didn't win a single full England cap. This is something that will shock and sadden those that saw him in his prime. Duncan was a wonderfully gifted, skilful forward, equally at home out wide or in a central position.

That he was class is beyond dispute – and he played for Mansfield Town! Born in Grimsby, but nurtured through the Nottingham Forest youth set-up, he twice moved to Field Mill for loan spells to gain experience.

He made 10 appearances in a Stags jersey, three as a substitute, during the latter part of the 1969–70 season. Forest were in desperate need of goalkeeping cover, so manager Tommy Eggleston allowed Dave Hollins to move to the City Ground in exchange for the 19-year-old striker.

His first start for the Stags couldn't have turned out much better. Strike partner Dudley Roberts scored three and Duncan netted two himself, in a rousing 5–0 win at home to Southport. His first league goal came from a well-anticipated rebound, after an initial effort had hit the crossbar.

He also scored against Rotherham United three days later, but, although keen to make the move permanent, Mansfield were unable to agree terms with Forest and Duncan went back at the end of his loan spell.

He had still not fully cemented himself in the Reds' first team three years later, and again came to Field Mill. This time he was a sensation, scoring seven goals in just six games, including a hat-trick against Bradford City.

Dave Mackay, the Forest boss, re-called Duncan and the player was then catapulted into the big time. He was signed by Brian Clough, during his brief stint as Leeds United boss, then moved to Anderlecht in Belgium before returning to the top-flight of English football with Everton.

Something of a 'media darling', Duncan was among the most charismatic players of his generation – with a party piece of leaping over a Mini car – but his footballing ability could never be underestimated.

Later in his career he played for both Chelsea and Blackburn Rovers, as well as spending time in the United States and Hong Kong. Nowadays, Duncan is a successful businessman, media pundit and popular after-dinner speaker.

Alfred Middleton

Date of birth: c.1890
Died: not known

Mansfield Town record:

Appearances: League 205, FA Cup 22, Others 26
Goals: League 103, FA Cup 10, Others 10
Debut: 4 September 1909 v Ilkeston United (h) lost 0–2

Also played for: Wesley, Mansfield Mechanics, Stockport County, Sutton Junction, Grantham

WHATEVER the era, whatever the opposition, it's still a major achievement to net over 100 league goals for a club. The first Stags player to do it was Alf Middleton.

A local lad, he made his first-team debut at the start of the 1909–10 season, wearing the number 10 shirt vacated by the highly popular Birmingham-bound Jack Needham. During the previous campaign Needham had netted 46 goals from just 35 league games, a club record.

Over the next decade and a half Middleton proved to be a more than adequate replacement, and an outstanding clubman. He could claim to be the only Mansfield player to have been with the club from the days when they were known as 'Wesley', right through to after World War One. Additionally, he would have sported the club's black and white colours before the hostilities and the amber and blue afterwards!

He briefly left the club during the 1912–13 season, signing for Stockport County in December for £65, but returned in the subsequent summer after being released. Otherwise, he was with the club for 14 years and played in three different leagues for them.

His most prolific season came just after the war, when he blasted 23 goals in 28 league matches to help the club claim the Central Alliance championship. He hit two league hat-tricks that season, one against Gresley Rovers and the other versus Grantham Town, to add to one he'd hit against Sutton Junction in 1916. On four separate occasions he was the leading scorer in the league and he was certainly a man for the special occasion.

Alf was selected to play in a representative match to reopen Field Mill after World War One and he scored both Mansfield goals in their first league match after normal games resumed. He also netted twice when the Stags played their first game against Worksop Town in the Midland League in August 1921.

A prolific goalscorer throughout his playing days, he netted a total of 104 league goals in his career with Wesley/Mansfield Town and a further nine for the Mechanics.

He was transferred to Sutton Junction in October 1921 and after a spell at Grantham he retired from playing in May 1925. To this day he remains fourth in the list of Mansfield's overall top scorers.

Johnny Miller

Date of birth: 21 September 1950, Ipswich

Mansfield Town record:

Appearances: League 113, FA Cup 6, League Cup 7
Goals: League 14, FA Cup 1, League Cup 1
Debut: 14 August 1976 v Scunthorpe Utd (h) won 2–0

Also played for: Ipswich Town, Norwich City, Port Vale, Oakham United, Blidworth Welfare

JOHNNY Miller was Peter Morris's first signing as the Stags' boss in the summer of 1976. The pair had previously been teammates at both Norwich City and Ipswich Town and the mutual respect they shared stood them in good stead as they helped clinch the Third Division title in their first season at Field Mill.

As Dave Smith's Championship-winning side began to break up, new faces were brought in to replace them. For Johnny the immediate task was awesome – filling Jimmy McCaffrey's berth on the wing. There's no doubt that Miller set about his task with relish. Always giving of his best, the man nicknamed 'Dusty' soon became a warm favourite himself.

Among the few players to be equally respected by the followers of both East Anglian clubs, Johnny had begun his senior career with Ipswich Town, signing for them on his 17th birthday. He made his senior debut in March 1969 and played a total of 60 first-team games for the Tractor Boys before his switch to Norfolk. The transfer fee of £43,000 still hadn't been exchanged when Miller netted twice for his new employers against his former club – imagine the furore!

While at Norwich City, Johnny helped capture promotion to the top flight in 1975 and made a losing trip to Wembley for the League Cup Final.

After his move to Mansfield Town, Johnny played in 40 of the 46 league games as the club recorded its second title in three seasons. Equally at home on either flank, he had pace to burn and possessed a powerful shot, scoring all five of his goals that season in the first half of the campaign.

Despite a run of niggling injuries, Johnny was a valued member of the side in the club's only season in the old Second Division, again scoring five times in the league, with an FA Cup winner at Plymouth for good measure.

Johnny moved to Port Vale in 1980 but returned to the Mansfield district after his professional playing days were at an end. He joined the staff at Ashfield District Council's Huthwaite Leisure Centre and continued to play good standard local non-league football into his mid-40s.

Charlie Mitten

Date of birth:	17 January 1921, Rangoon, Burma
Died:	2 January 2002

Mansfield Town record:

Player-manager:	1956–1958
Appearances:	League 100, FA Cup 6
Goals:	League 25, FA Cup 2
Debut:	4 February 1956 v Wrexham (h) won 6–1

Also played for: Manchester United, Santa Fe (Colombia), Fulham

Also managed: Newcastle United

CHARLIE Mitten was a footballing pioneer – a maverick whose career earned him condemnation and plaudits in equal measure. That he should ever have appeared at Field Mill is extraordinary in itself but, at the age of 35, in February 1956, he joined the Stags as player-manager.

He played exactly 100 league games for Mansfield Town, plus another six in the FA Cup, scoring 25 league goals, plus two FA Cup goals, all from the outside-left position. Charlie stayed with the club for over two years, leaving in June 1958 to become manager of Newcastle United.

Mitten had risen to fame at Manchester United, where he scored 50 league goals in 142 appearances, and another 11 goals in cup competitions. His finest moment was playing a part in the 1947–48 FA Cup-winning side under Matt Busby, beating a Blackpool side that included Stanley Matthews and Stan Mortensen by 4–2 after trailing 2–1 with 20 minutes left.

He was known as something of a 'penalty king' and once scored a hat-trick of spot-kicks in a First Division match against Aston Villa. He left Old Trafford in 1950 to join Santa Fe in Bogotà, Colombia, with a signing-on fee reputed to be in the region of £5,000, a flat and a car. This was a controversial move because Colombia did not belong to FIFA and hence Mitten was considered a football outlaw. Charlie became known as the 'Bogotà Bandit'.

After a season in Colombia, he, along with all of the other foreign players, was forced to leave. On return to England, he was banned for 18 months for having gone to Colombia, and then he joined Fulham, prior to his move to Mansfield.

His close control was a delight to watch and he did improve the club's fortunes, making several astute signings as well as scoring some important goals. Mitten's son John also played for the Stags – just three games as a 16-year-old while his father was in charge – although they did not play in the same side.

John followed his father to Newcastle in 1958, and later also played for Plymouth and Exeter, as well as playing county cricket for Leicestershire.

Charlie Mitten died on 2 January 2002 at the age of 80.

Peter Morris

Date of birth: 8 November 1943, New Houghton, Derbyshire

Mansfield Town record:

Appearances: League 328, FA Cup 19, League Cup 18
Goals: League 53
Debut: 24 February 1961 v Workington (a) won 3–1
Player-Manager: July 1976–February 1978

Also played for: Ipswich Town, Norwich City

Also managed: Peterborough United, Crewe Alexandra, Southend, Boston United, Kettering, Kings Lynn

PETER Morris enjoyed two spells at Field Mill. As a youngster he'd joined the club at 15 and gone on to skipper the side. Later, he returned for his first crack at management.

As a schoolboy, Peter trained at Mansfield Town two evenings a week. Sam Weaver, manager at the time, offered him a place on the ground staff and he was in the reserves at just 16. A keen fan anyway, Peter was in his element. 'I'd been watching the club regularly since I was about 10. Like all schoolboys I'd got my heroes – Sammy Chapman was one, so too George Darwin, an inside-forward who was quick as lightning.'

Weaver's departure from the club brought in Raich Carter, who believed in giving youth a chance. Peter, along with fellow 17-year-olds Mike Stringfellow and Ken Wagstaff, was handed a debut at Workington in February 1961.

'Raich gave me a run in the side of about a dozen matches, then said I needed a break. I was back the following season, with added responsibility. I was still just 17 but was appointed the club's penalty-taker.'

Morris scored 10 goals that season, nine from the spot – a high ratio, as he explains: 'We used to get quite a lot of penalty kicks because "Waggy" was always getting brought down!'

While still only 18, Peter skippered the side for the first time and became an integral cog in the Stags midfield for eight seasons, making almost 300 league appearances. The chance to play at a higher level couldn't be refused him, but there was general anger when he was eventually allowed to move to Ipswich Town for just £15,000. Peter enjoyed a successful playing career with the Suffolk side, and then Norwich City, whom he joined in June 1974.

His chance to return 'home' arose in the summer of 1976, when he was appointed the player-manager of Mansfield Town after Dave Smith had been controversially axed. 'I inherited a fine side from Dave', Peter accepted. 'There were some really good players at the club but we still needed strengthening and I used a few contacts to bring players to the club.'

The arrival of Ernie Moss kick-started the charge towards the title, secured on the final day at Wrexham. 'That was a memorable day', says the former Stags boss. 'But people forget, there were plenty of other good performances, which got us in that position.'

With Stags struggling in Division Two, the following season Peter accepted an offer to become assistant manager at Newcastle United. Over the next two decades Peter enjoyed a hugely successful career in management, at a succession of lower league or non-league clubs.

Ernie Moss

Date of birth: 19 October 1949, Chesterfield

Mansfield Town record:

Appearances: League 57, FA Cup 0, League Cup 2
Goals: League 21, FA Cup 0, League Cup 0
Debut: 18 December 1976 v Wrexham (h) won 2–0

Also played for: Chesterfield, Peterborough, Port Vale, Lincoln City, Doncaster Rovers, Stockport County, Scarborough, Rochdale, Kettering Town, Boston United

IT'S fairly uncommon for a player to be held in such high esteem by both Chesterfield and Stags fans, but Ernie Moss was no ordinary footballer.

He earns his place as a Mansfield Town legend for his goal-scoring feats during the second half of the 1976–77 Division Three Championship-winning season. Ernie's 13 goals from just 29 appearances, after signing for £18,000 from Peterborough United, helped clinch the title.

'Big Ern', as he was affectionately known, fitted in at Field Mill immediately, helped by having another former Spireite, Kevin Randall, as his strike partner. Moss had to wait until his third match for his new club before getting off the mark but the goal, against Port Vale, still stands out high among his memories. 'An attempted clearance had struck the referee and fell to me' he remembers. 'Just as I hit the ball John Ridley, a Vale defender, came across and caught me with a tackle but I'd just got my shot away in time and it flew into the top corner.'

That strike began a goalscoring spree which saw him find the opposition net in six consecutive games. A hugely successful campaign saw the Stags elevated to the Second Division for the first time. Having clinched promotion already, Stags went to Wrexham on the final day of the season, needing a win to claim the title. The added ingredient was that the home side needed the points to go up as well.

'For much of that game Wrexham hammered us. Rod Arnold had taken a knock and we were trying to protect our 'keeper as much as anything, then in the last minute we got a break. Kevin Randall pulled the ball back and I whacked it in. Our players and all the fans just went bananas!'

Sadly, Ernie missed much of the next season through injury. Having suffered with a pelvic problem for some time, the striker was forced to undergo surgery on both hips. The fans still feel that the club would have avoided relegation had their big striker been fit that season.

When he did return to the fold a new manager had been installed. 'Billy Bingham clearly didn't rate me and it was obvious I wasn't part of his plans.' A return to Chesterfield materialised in January 1979, but not before Ernie had scored his final goal for the club – and certainly the most bizarre.

'Mike Walker, later to manage Norwich and Everton, was in goal for Colchester. He came out of his area to give the ball to his left-back. The defender tried to clear up the field but, as I turned away, the ball struck my backside and flew back into the unprotected goal!'

Ernie carried on – and on – and on with his playing career. At the age of 44 he became the oldest player to score in the Conference, when he netted for Kettering.

For over 20 years now Ernie Moss has owned and run a sports shop in Chesterfield, but he is still heavily involved in the game. At the end of the 2003–04 season he celebrated his third season as manager of Matlock Town by leading them to the runners-up spot in the Unibond First Division. A switch of club saw Ernie take charge at Hucknall Town in readiness for the 2004–05 season.

Malcolm Partridge

Date of birth: 28 August 1950, Calow, near Chesterfield

Mansfield Town record:

Appearances:	League 67, FA Cup 6, League Cup 6
Goals:	League 20, FA Cup 2, League Cup 3
Debut:	11 March 1968 v Bristol Rovers (h) won 3–0

Also played for: Leicester City, Charlton Athletic, Grimsby Town, Scunthorpe United

THE first Mansfield Town player to score a hat-trick in the League Cup competition was Malcolm Partridge. As it came against local rivals Chesterfield, it was especially sweet for the Calow-born forward.

Malcolm's best moments in a Stags jersey came on the evening of 19 August 1970. The pick of his goals in that match is still part of the club's folklore – a 52nd-minute drive from the corner of the box that rocketed into the top corner beyond the startled 'keeper.

The Stags won that match 6–2, thus setting up a second-round home clash against Liverpool. Partridge lined up against Bill Shankly's side and played his part in an entertaining 0–0 draw. He was denied an opportunity of being around for the replay at Anfield Road, though, as Leicester City stepped in to sign the youngster for £50,000, a Stags record at the time.

Malcolm had played in just 79 senior games for the Stags, netting 25 times. He had been given his opportunity early, making his first-team debut aged just 17 years 196 days, and he marked the occasion with a goal.

He began in a central striking role but eventually moved out to the right wing, making the number seven shirt his own. His best season for Mansfield, in 1969–70, brought him 13 goals in the league.

Malcolm's penultimate league appearance for the Stags also brought joy to the many supporters who followed the club to Villa Park to see the first-ever league clash against Aston Villa. He scored the only goal, his last for the Town, to provide a fitting send-off.

After leaving Field Mill many expected Malcolm to go on and play at the very top level of the game. He did help Leicester City to the Second Division title in 1971 but his time with the Foxes wasn't regarded as a great success.

After a short loan spell at Charlton Athletic he joined Grimsby Town in March 1975 and enjoyed the most consistent spell of his career. In his three and a half years with the Mariners he scored 24 goals in 134 first-team appearances. He moved to Scunthorpe United in the summer of 1979, playing close to 100 matches for them before entering the non-league game with Skegness Town.

Malcolm's son Scott also became a professional footballer, playing for a number of clubs including Bristol City, Brentford, Torquay United and Cardiff City.

Sandy Pate

Date of birth: 15 August 1944, Lennox Castle, Glasgow

Mansfield Town record:

Appearances: League 413, FA Cup 36, League Cup 22
Goals: League 2, FA Cup 0, League Cup 1
Debut: 13 October 1967 v Stockport County (a) lost 0–1

Also played for: Watford

TO A generation of Mansfield Town followers, the number two jersey meant one name – Sandy Pate. The Scottish right-back served under six managers during a Field Mill playing career which spanned a dozen years.

Sandy made 471 appearances for the club, a record that stood until it was overtaken by teammate and good friend, Rod Arnold. Amazingly, the Scot was an ever-present in the side between 21 September 1968 and 26 April 1975, a run of 366 consecutive appearances.

'The longer the run went on, the more I wanted to keep it going', says Sandy. 'I once pulled a quad muscle on my right leg. It was agony but they wanted to put me through a late fitness test. John Haselden, the coach, put the ball down for a goal-kick and asked me to kick it as far as I could. The ball didn't get out of the area! That was it as far as I was concerned. Suddenly the club doctor appeared and 15 minutes before kick-off I was given an injection. Somehow I got through the game!'

The Scot, though, was far more than just a regular performer – he was a leader and an inspiration to those around him. He'd played as a right winger in his younger days but was converted to right-back upon joining Watford in 1965, a decision that eventually led to Sandy moving to Mansfield. Ken Furphy, a right-back himself, was Watford's player-manager and he had designs on Sandy becoming his long-term replacement.

'Ken was 38 and I was playing well for the reserves. Then he pointed out that he was only 23 games away from his 500th appearance and wanted to reach that milestone. I didn't want to hang around for six months while he achieved it.'

Tommy Eggleston, the Stags boss, stepped in to sign the Scot but it was another member of staff who helped find him digs. 'Sam Weaver, Tommy's assistant, made arrangements for me to stay at his brother's house at Pleasley. The welcome I got there, and the friendship, made me realise I'd made the right move.'

Sandy became a permanent fixture in the side, enjoying the best period in the Town's history. 'It was just a great period to be involved with the club. Apart from league success, we had some terrific draws in the cup competitions. The fans enjoy those big games and as players we certainly did as well.'

The crowning moment of Sandy's Field Mill career was captaining the 1974–75 side to the Fourth Division Championship, but he also fondly recalls the three goals he managed to score for the Stags, though not with complete clarity. 'My first was against Sheffield Wednesday, at home. I just hit the ball in low from the right. Somehow it beat everybody and went in the corner!'

His long run in the side ended at the start of the 1975–76 season. An ankle injury, picked up in training, ruled him out of the season opener but he returned soon after, making 41 league appearances that season. Sandy scored his only other league goal on his final home appearance, against Orient, and played his final game for the club the following week, at Walsall, in May 1978.

Remaining in the Mansfield area, Sandy spent several years as a publican before taking over the managerial role at non-league Rainworth Miners Welfare.

Lee Peacock

Date of birth: 9 October 1976, Paisley, Scotland

Mansfield Town record:

Appearances: League 89, FA Cup 4, League Cup 4, Others 4
Goals: League 29, FA Cup 0, League Cup 1, Others 2
Debut: 18 October 1997 v Macclesfield Town (a) lost 0–1

Also played for: Carlisle United, Manchester City, Bristol City, Sheffield Wednesday

WHEN it was announced that the Stags would be spending a club record £150,000 on a young striker from Carlisle United, many supporters were a little mystified. Just who was he and why was he so expensive?

Over Lee Peacock's two years at Field Mill, he was to become a big crowd favourite and it came as no surprise when he was eventually transferred for a healthy profit to Manchester City.

Peacock made his Stags debut when coming on as a second-half substitute away at Macclesfield Town in October 1997. With virtually his first touch he hit the Macclesfield woodwork.

His first of many goals in a Mansfield Town shirt came in the 3–2 home win over Scarborough the following month and his second was a powerhouse of a header away at Peterborough United.

From then on in, goals were his business. In the 1998–99 season, Lee scored 19 goals in 51 appearances, in all competitions. Some of those 19 goals were special, like the deflected free-kick that helped the Stags claim an improbable away win, ironically against Manchester City, in the Autoglass Trophy.

The goals he will perhaps be best remembered for were the three he scored at home, on a Friday night, against Barnet. Certainly they should have been the clearest to see – it was the first Football League match to be played with the new luminous football!

He hit one other hat-trick for Town, against Peterborough, a month before being sold. His performances were attracting the scouts from the bigger clubs and it was only a matter of time before the latest Field Mill goalscoring hero was on his way. On 26 October 1999, he signed for Manchester City for £500,000.

Stags supporters were sad to see him go, but accepted it as part of the financial reality of life at a lower league club.

Strangely it never worked out for Peacock at Maine Road and after just eight league appearances he was transferred to Bristol City, where he has once again became a proven goalscorer. During the summer of 2004 he transferred to Sheffield Wednesday.

Very few ex-players earn respect from their former football club's supporters, but Lee Peacock is one of those that has. Who knows what the future will hold for him? At Mansfield Town though, the gelled hair, tattoos and the goals will be remembered for quite a few years to come.

Kevin Pilkington

Date of birth: 8 March 1974, Hitchin

Mansfield Town record (to end of season 2003–04):

Appearances: League 125, FA Cup 9, League Cup 3, Others 5
Debut: 1 May 2001 v Darlington (h) won 3–2

Also played for: Manchester United, Rochdale, Rotherham United, Port Vale

MANSFIELD Town haven't had too many goalkeeper-captains down the years and they certainly haven't had too many ex-Manchester United players on their staff. They also haven't had many footballers as dedicated to their profession as Kevin Pilkington. Teammate Liam Lawrence was asked to write the pen portraits for the Stags players in the official match programme for the 2004 play-off final. He described Kevin as being 'Mr Serious!'

'I said to him afterwards, 'Why not just put 'Boring Old ****?', says the big goalie. 'He knows I like to laugh and joke as much as anybody but I feel there's a time to relax and a time to work. Footballers are extremely lucky. We only have to work for three or four hours a day so why not stay focussed and work hard during that time?'

It's that attitude that prompted manager Keith Curle to appoint Kevin as the club captain, shortly after taking over the reins. 'He just pulled me to one side and told me to take the armband. I feel I'm a good pro and it's nice to have that recognition from others.'

At just 16 years of age Kevin was spotted playing for Harrowby United, in Grantham. 'The Manchester United scouts were looking for a goalkeeper for their Under-16 side and I was delighted to sign schoolboy forms.'

There were a few illustrious names among Kevin's contempories at Old Trafford. 'I played in the same 1992 FA Youth Cup-winning side as David Beckham, Gary Neville and Nicky Butt.'

Understudying Peter Schmeichel was a hugely beneficial experience for Kev and he made the odd appearance. 'I played eight times for United's first team', he recalls, savouring every moment. 'The highlight undoubtedly was my debut, at Old Trafford, against Crystal Palace, in front of 55,000 people!'

In search of first-team football Kev was loaned the length and breadth of the land, and even north of the border. 'I actually spent three months at Celtic but didn't get a game!' The frustration of inactivity has long been forgotten, with Kevin clocking up over a century of appearances for the Stags. 'I've loved my time at Mansfield', he says. 'I had a difficult spell during the 2003–04 season when my dad, Tony, passed away. He had been a great inspiration and I was missing him dreadfully but the fans stuck by me and I'll always be grateful.'

Towards the end of that season Kev was to feel mixed emotions as Mansfield won a play-off semi-final and then lost the final, both on penalty shoot-outs. 'If the 'keeper has a little bit of luck you can be a hero in those situations. The luck was missing at Cardiff!'

Captain Kev led the side with pride at the Millennium Stadium – a truly dedicated professional.

Cyril Poole

Date of birth: 13 March 1921, Forest Town, Mansfield, Nottinghamshire
Died: 11 February 1996

Mansfield Town record:

Appearances: League 16
Goals: League 1
Debut: 27 February 1937 v New Brighton (h) lost 2–3

Also played for: Notts CCC and England (cricket)

WHEN local lad Cyril Poole made his debut against New Brighton on 27 February 1937, he became the youngest ever, at 15 years and 351 days, to play for Mansfield Town.

The fair-haired youngster had been signed on amateur terms, after shining alongside the seniors in Annesley Colliery's side. Jack Roy, a speedy left-winger, had been sold to Sheffield Wednesday and firstly 16-year-old Roy Briggs, and then Poole were given their chance.

Sadly, there was to be no fairytale success for the slightly-built Poole on his debut – the Stags went down 3–2. His next league game for the club, more than 12 years later, came during the 1949–50 season. The gap between first and second appearances is also believed to be a unique achievement.

By the time of his return to wearing the Stags' colours Cyril Poole had established himself as an outstanding county cricketer. After performing consistently for Mansfield Colliery in the Bassetlaw League, he went on to sign for Nottinghamshire County Cricket Club and played in 366 first-class matches for them. Between 1948 and 1962 he amassed 18,685 runs, hitting 24 centuries, with a career best score of 222 not out.

A left-handed batsman and occasional left-arm bowler, he went on the 1951–52 tour of India and appeared in three Test matches for England, making a top score of 69 not out.

During the war years Cyril had continued to play football, guesting for the Stags, Chesterfield, Nottingham Forest and Sheffield United before joining Gillingham, still a non-league club at the time. He helped the Kent side to the Southern League Championship in both 1947 and 1949, with a runners-up spot in 1948.

On 5 September 1949 Poole returned to the Mansfield Town starting line-up and scored in a 3–3 away draw at York City. This was to be his only senior goal for the club.

During the next couple of seasons he featured occasionally, usually at either left-back or on the left wing. In all, he made 17 appearances for the club. After being released by the Stags he signed for Corby Town but was then chosen to go on tour with the England cricketers so didn't play for them. Instead, upon his return he opted to continue his footballing career with non-league Clipstone Welfare.

Cyril's cousin, Billy Wheatley, made a total of 41 first-team appearances for the Stags between 1948 and 1950.

Johnny Quigley

Date of birth: 28 June 1935, Glasgow

Mansfield Town record:

Appearances: League 105, FA Cup 13, League Cup 4
Goals: League 2, FA Cup 0, League Cup 0
Debut: 10 August 1968 v Brighton & Hove Albion (a) won 2–1

Also played for: Nottingham Forest, Huddersfield Town, Bristol City

CAPTAIN of the 1968–69 FA Cup giant-killing side was Scotsman Johnny Quigley. He was a tough-tackling inside-forward, or midfielder as they are known nowadays. His all-round game was impressive, he was comfortable in possession, he was a fine distributor of the ball and he displayed sound tactical acumen.

Johnny had spent the bulk of his career at Nottingham Forest, where he made over 230 appearances. The highlight of his time at the City Ground came in May 1959, when he played in the FA Cup Final victory over Luton Town at Wembley Stadium. He returned to play in the famous old stadium just a few months later, in the Charity Shield.

Many seasoned observers felt that he was capable of going on to earn full international honours with his country but Scotland had plenty of options in those days and the player's ambition remained unfulfilled.

After leaving Forest Johnny joined Huddersfield Town, where he remained for about 18 months. He then saw out a similar spell at Bristol City, later claiming to have enjoyed his time at Ashton Gate as much as any in his career.

Tommy Eggleston signed Johnny Quigley in the summer of 1968 and immediately made him club skipper. Wearing the number four jersey, the new captain was a revelation. Hugely popular in the dressing room, he had the respect of his teammates, on and off the field. He was a real leader, a true captain.

He was an ever-present in his first season, scoring just twice – both away from home, in games at Hartlepool and Tranmere. More than his goals though, he and his side will be remembered for the successive cup runs, to the sixth round in 1968–69 and to the fifth round the following season.

In November 1970 the club had a bit of a re-shuffle. Johnny, keen to get into coaching, was appointed as player/coach under new manager Jock Basford. Phil Waller became club skipper.

Despite Johnny's new title, he wasn't to play first-team football again. His final match had been a 3-2 home victory over Halifax Town.

One year after his appointment, both Basford and Quigley were sacked, after a run of poor results. It was a sad way for Johnny to end his association with Mansfield Town.

Johnny then accepted an offer to continue his coaching career in the Middle East, where he remained for many years.

Kevin Randall

Date of birth: 20 August 1945, Ashton-under-Lyne, Lancashire

Mansfield Town record:

Appearances: League 66, FA Cup 4, League Cup 1
Goals: League 20, FA Cup 1, League Cup 0
Debut: 15 November 1975 v Grimsby Town (a) lost 1–4

Also played for: Bury, Chesterfield, Notts County, York City, Alfreton Town, Goole Town

Managed: York City, Chesterfield

KEVIN Randall spent just a small part of his playing career at Field Mill but his goals helped cement promotion to the second tier of our domestic game for the only time in the club's history. He joined the Stags after establishing himself as a prolific goalscorer at both Chesterfield and Notts County and later returned to Mansfield for a four-year stint as youth development officer.

Lancashire-born, Kevin might well have spent a lucrative career as a Manchester United player. His schools football had been spent playing for Droylsden and Ashton-under-Lyne and he was invited to Old Trafford for training. He played for United's junior side and made several appearances at 'B' team level.

Opportunities, however, were always going to be at a premium and he chose to join Bury for a chance of league football. After just eight months at Gigg Lane he moved to Chesterfield. During a six-year stay at Saltergate, Kevin scored over a century of goals from almost 300 outings. His strike partnership with Ernie Moss was among the most feared in the lower leagues.

His move to Notts County brought over 40 goals in 125 appearances, so when he joined the Stags in November 1975, they could truly claim to have bought a proven goalscorer. Kev's first 12 months at Mansfield were steady, rather than spectacular. He hit the headlines, though, in November 1976 when he scored all four goals in a 4–0 home win over Reading. A month later manager Peter Morris completed the signing of Ernie Moss from Peterborough United. The old Randall–Moss partnership was back in action and just as lethal as ever. In only their second match back together Kevin scored the only goal in a 1–0 win at Chesterfield – a result guaranteed to make any Stags fan purr with delight!

With two in-form strikers Mansfield won the Third Division title – Randall's 17 league goals the leading contribution. Somewhat surprisingly, the manager chose not to select Kevin for the early part of the next season and, even more surprisingly in most people's view, he was allowed to sign for York City. At Bootham Crescent he played, coached and even had a spell as caretaker manager.

After short periods in and out of the non-league game, and a brief stint back at Chesterfield as manager, Kevin returned to Field Mill to join the backroom staff. He then went back to Saltergate as assistant to John Duncan before joining the coaching staff at Sheffield United.

Football is a team game but individual achievements are important and Kevin Randall's goals lifted Mansfield Town to the highest level in their history.

Dudley Roberts

Date of birth: 16 October 1945, Derby

Mansfield Town record:

Appearances: League 200, FA Cup 19, League Cup 10
Goals: League 66, FA Cup 6, League Cup 1
Debut: 16 March 1968 v Brighton & Hove Albion (a) lost 0–3

Also played for: Coventry City, Doncaster Rovers, Scunthorpe United

MANSFIELD Town have had their share of decent strikers over the years. Few, if any, possessed such natural heading ability as Dudley Roberts. Not for nothing did the fans christen him 'Deadly Dud!'

He made his debut on the same afternoon as three other new signings – Phil Waller, Nick Sharkey and Jimmy Goodfellow – as manager Tommy Eggleston looked to freshen up his squad. Roberts had been signed from Coventry City, where his father Ted had been a great pre-war centre forward. Dud's heading ability was already the talk of the 'circuit' and Eggleston wanted to use him as a target man. Little did he realise how successful a ploy it would become.

Over the next six years Dud scored 73 goals for the club, as well as setting up dozens more for his appreciative colleagues. With 18 league goals in 1969–70 and 22 the following year, he twice topped the club's goalscoring charts.

Like his teammates, he enjoyed his moment of fame. Dudley scored the first Mansfield goal in the 1969 FA Cup victory over West Ham United. The 22nd-minute strike was a simple close-range side-footer after a flowing build-up. Norman Giller, writing in the *Daily Express*, described the goal thus: 'Goodfellow released the ball towards Roberts, loitering with intent at the far post. He swiftly pulled it under control and steered his shot into the net.'

His aerial dominance and prodigious leaping ability claimed many important goals for the club but twice he was harshly penalised for getting up so high – both in important matches. In the FA Cup fifth round tie with Leeds United in 1970, with the scores still level, Dudley's towering climb above defender Paul Reaney gave Jimmy Goodfellow a simple tap-in. To the stunned amazement of the Stags players the referee disallowed the goal for an unwarranted pushing offence.

Later the same year a similar occurrence denied Mansfield a famous victory over Liverpool at Field Mill. No one, bar the referee, felt that there had been any infringement committed when Dudley scored what should have been a late winner.

Although he spent most of his career 'up front', Dud was always happy to help out in defence and played several games for the Stags at centre-half and even at right-back, during a rare occasion when Sandy Pate was out injured.

Roberts netted three hat-tricks for the Stags, including one in a game against Tranmere Rovers, in 1971, when he scored four altogether. They were great days! He later played for both Doncaster Rovers and Scunthorpe United but settled in the Mansfield area after his playing days were over.

Mick Saxby

Date of birth: 12 August 1957, Mansfield

Mansfield Town record:

Appearances: League 79, FA Cup 2, League Cup 2
Goals: League 5, FA Cup 0, League Cup 0
Debut: 14 February 1976 v Halifax Town (a) won 2–1

Also played for: Luton Town, Grimsby Town, Lincoln City, Middlesbrough

AS A rookie pro Mick Saxby learned that life as a footballer can be very cruel. The youngster fulfilled an early ambition by joining his home-town club and getting an opportunity in the first team at just 18 years of age. 'I made my debut away at Halifax', he fondly recalls. 'We were struggling at the bottom of the league – in fact I think we needed snookers to stay up! Anyway, I got the winner, heading in a late corner from Gordon Hodgson. I was dropped the following week and didn't play again that year as the side went on a long unbeaten run.'

The following season a few more opportunities came his way – 10, in fact, precisely the number required to collect one of the Division Three Championship medals the side had claimed. 'I'd enjoyed all the celebrations, as a fan, a couple of years earlier and now to be playing alongside some of my heroes, and to win a medal myself, was just unbelievable.'

One of the most popular and jovial characters ever to play for the club, the big central defender became a cult figure on the terraces. Younger brother Gary graduated through the Field Mill ranks at around the same time and both Saxbys often found themselves in the same starting line-up. 'People used to say that between us we'd have made a great player', says Mick. 'My game was probably more about heart and commitment, whereas Gary had all the skill and was equally good with both feet.'

During the 1978–79 season Mick was an ever-present and a worthy recipient of the club's Player of the Year award. It was to be his last season at Field Mill prior to a contentious move to Luton Town, set up while manager Billy Bingham was holidaying in Australia.

'There was talk of Leeds, Derby and Sunderland all being interested in signing me but Luton came forward with an offer and when I drove down and met up with David Pleat the deal seemed too good to refuse.' After two and a half years at Luton Mick sustained an injury to his right knee while playing against Crystal Palace. Surgery was needed to save his career.

'The club found a surgeon, up in Scotland, who was rated as the best in his field. The trouble was, he was very elderly but agreed to do one more operation before he retired – on me! The Luton physio attended and he told me afterwards that, at one stage, the old boy had to ask for a chair to sit down and have a rest!'

Although Mick was able to play again he couldn't perform to the same standards as before the injury. 'Basically, I was never the same again. I ended up having 11 operations in all and although I played for a few other clubs I was eventually told to pack it in while I could still walk.'

Mick spent a short time as the Commercial Manager at Field Mill before embarking on a career with the *Nottingham Evening Post*. Still a regular at Field Mill, his forthright and entertaining views on the game have often been put to good use as a radio match summariser.

Albert Scanlon

Date of birth: 10 October 1935, Manchester

Mansfield Town record:

Appearances: League 108, FA Cup 3, League Cup 5
Goals: League 21, FA Cup 0, League Cup 3
Debut: 3 April 1963 v Bradford City (a) won 3–1

Also played for: Manchester United, Newcastle United, Lincoln City

JUST over five years after surviving the Munich air disaster, Albert Scanlon became a Stag. The tricky left-winger was one of the original Busby Babes, winning the FA Youth Cup in both 1953 and 1954. He sustained serious head and leg injuries in the crash but recovered in time to play all 42 league games of the 1958–59 season, helping Manchester United to runners-up position in the league.

The following season his form became a little more inconsistent and United sold him, for £17,500, to Newcastle United. The Magpies boss, at the time, was Charlie Mitten, a former Mansfield Town player-manager, who also happened to be Albert's uncle.

Albert played just 22 times for Newcastle before moving to Lincoln City. A year later he was at Field Mill, becoming new boss Tommy Cummings's first signing. His Mansfield career got off to a terrific start with goals in three of his first four matches, including a debut strike at Bradford City.

Despite a decrease in his once-blistering pace, he proved to be a steady and reliable performer for the Stags, helping them to promotion in his first season and to third place in Division Three a couple of years later.

For a wide player, Albert netted with a fair amount of regularity and a League Cup winner against Birmingham City set up a tie at West Ham United in the third round. The star-studded East Enders won 4–0. Mansfield would gain their revenge in the not-too-distant future.

At the end of the 1965–66 season Albert was released and signed for non-league Belper Town. He later moved back to the north-west, settling in Salford. He fell on hard times for a while but Manchester United undertook to look after their 'Busby Babes' with a series of benefits and a testimonial game.

During the early part of his career Scanlon had been capped five times for the England Under-23 side but he was unable to continue his early progress, mainly due to the events of 6 February 1958. Speaking later about the crash, Scanlon, who had been unconscious in a Munich hospital for five days with a fractured skull, said, 'When I woke up I was on a ward with five of the team. I started wondering where all of the others were, and asked a priest. Eventually he said to me "What you see is what you've got. There's nobody else, everyone's dead!"'

Dominic Sharkey

Date of birth: 4 May 1943, Helensburgh, Dunbartonshire

Mansfield Town record:

Appearances: League 69, FA Cup 7, League Cup 4
Goals: League 17, FA Cup 4, League Cup 0
Debut: 16 March 1968 v Brighton & Hove Albion (a) lost 0–3

Also played for: Sunderland, Leicester City, Hartlepool United, South Shields

ALTHOUGH Dominic Sharkey was the club's leading goalscorer for a season he, like Ray Keeley, earns his plaudits as a Mansfield Town legend for one single goal as much as anything.

Rounding off the Stags' incredible victory over West Ham United in 1969 was Nick, with the third goal in our 3–0 win. Pouncing on a 49th-minute error from 'keeper Bobby Ferguson, the diminutive striker pounced to drive the ball home.

Sharkey had joined Mansfield Town in March 1968, moving from Leicester City for £10,000 after a brief spell at Filbert Street which, nevertheless, yielded five goals from six appearances. He scored his first Stags goals on just his second appearance, netting both in a 2–1 win at Vicarage Road, against Watford.

These were to be his only goals that season for the club but he was more prolific the following term. With Dudley Roberts and Bob Ledger supplying the more 'muscular' presence, at 5ft 6in tall Nick helped himself to 13 goals in the league, just outscoring his taller strike partners.

He also helped himself to another four in the FA Cup and held his place in the first team until midway through the following season. Handed a free transfer, he returned to the north-east to join Hartlepool United for a couple of seasons before leaving the professional game to play for South Shields.

Although born in Scotland, Nick went through the junior ranks at Sunderland and was only 16 when he made his league debut for the club, ironically due to the serious knee injury which ended Brian Clough's playing career. Between 1960 and 1967 he scored 62 goals in 117 appearances for the north-eastern club and earned Scottish international recognition at both youth and Under-23 level.

The name of Dominic Sharkey can still be found in football's record books. Playing for Sunderland against Norwich City on 20 February 1962 he scored five goals in a 7–1 victory at Roker Park in the old Second Division. This is still the joint-highest tally of goals for the Wearside club in a league game. Dominic is still idolised by the Sunderland supporters and is a popular and regular matchday visitor to the Stadium of Light.

Dave Smith

Date of birth: 22 September 1933, Dundee

Mansfield Town record:

Manager: April 1974–April 1976

Played for: Burnley, Brighton and Hove Albion, Bristol City

Also managed: Southend United, Plymouth Argyle, Dundee United, Torquay United

THE record books show that Dave Smith was manager of Mansfield Town for almost exactly two years. What they don't show was the impact he made on the town as a whole, not just at the football club.

To this day, there is still a feeling of anger and betrayal that Smith was sacked by a panicky Board of Directors. True, Mansfield were languishing in the lower depths of the table at the time, but most clubs need to adjust after securing promotion the previous year. And what a promotion campaign it had been – with the bonus of the Championship as well, the first title the club had ever won.

Dave's playing career had been spent as a full back at Burnley, Brighton and Bristol City before he turned to coaching. He had gathered experience in spells with Sheffield Wednesday, Newcastle United and Arsenal and was ready for his first crack at management when Danny Williams left the Mansfield post to move to Swindon.

Williams's appointment at the County Ground had, indirectly, led to Ray Clarke moving in the opposite direction. Clarke was to be one of Smith's key signings, as was Gordon Hodgson, a gloriously talented midfielder who was mysteriously allowed to leave Newcastle United.

Dave was inspirational as a manager and his players responded accordingly. Cumulatively, they were one of the best sides the club have ever fielded, but good sides have failed before.

The canny Scot masterminded a campaign that began with four straight league wins, saw them win 10 out of 11 at the turn of the year, and ended, at home, with a 7–0 drubbing of Scunthorpe United. The team maintained Championship form throughout the season.

While his players duly celebrated their achievements, Dave remained in the background, content with a job well done. Mansfield Town were on the map – and on the telly. His side had dominated a losing fifth round FA Cup tie against Carlisle United – then a top-flight outfit. The *Match of the Day* cameras were present to give a watching nation the chance to see how good the Stags had become.

Almost as soon as he'd arrived at Field Mill, however, the new 'messiah' had gone, allowed to leave a club he was on the threshold of turning into something big. Peter Morris completed the progression into Division Two but many feel that 'Smithy' knew what he was doing and would have taken the club even further. Sadly, we'll never know what might have been.

Dave joined Southend United as their new manager and took them to promotion in his second season. He later added a further promotion campaign to his CV with success at Plymouth Argyle.

In the right place at the right time – or one of the best managers the game has ever seen – the jury is still out, except among Stags fans!

Tom Smith

Date of birth: c.1896 Mansfield

Died: Not known

Mansfield Town record:

Appearances: League 153, FA Cup 13

Goals: League 1, FA Cup 0

Debut: 13 November 1915 v Sutton Junction (a) lost 2–3

MOST local clubs nowadays only survive by the strength of their membership, their loyal servants, one and all, for whom their particular sporting affiliation will last a lifetime. They will stand by their chosen side in times of good and bad.

Mansfield Town have had their share of devoted patrons over the course of the last century. Few have as much cause to be recognised as Tom Smith. A local lad, he fell in love with the club from a very early age and never considered moving his affections elsewhere.

More than just an avid fan, Tom was a decent player. He was a left-back, who stands comparison with many of the greats that have succeeded him in that position.

His exact date of birth is uncertain but he was in his 19th year when he broke into the first team. Like so many of his generation his ambitions were put on hold for the duration of World War One. When peace returned Tom was happy to take his place in a Mansfield Town side full of ambition. He was the only ever-present as the side romped to the Central Alliance title.

Over the next eight seasons Tom served the club he loved so much with dedicated professionalism and pride. As the side became more competitive he wasn't always certain of a starting place – but he never complained. He talked with great emotion about his only goal for the club – away, against Hull City reserves, in the Midland Counties League.

During 1925 he was appointed Mansfield Town's reserve team coach. Far from accepting this as being the end of his playing career he bounced back with renewed enthusiasm and quickly recovered his first-team berth.

His association with the club knew no boundaries and his medal collection reflected the longevity of his career. He won one league title, with a runners-up position to add, he twice played in Notts FA Senior Cup winning sides, he twice won the Mansfield Hospital Charity Cup, he won the Midland Combination Cup and the Notts Benevolent Bowl.

After making more than 150 league appearances, he finally hung up his boots and went back to supporting the side with fervour. Tom Smith dedicated his life to serving Mansfield Town.

Freddie Speed

Date of birth: 1909, Newcastle on Tyne

Mansfield Town record:

Appearances: League 100, FA Cup 10, League Cup 4
Goals: League 6, FA Cup 0, League Cup 0
Debut: 29 August 1936 v Barrow (h) won 2–1

Also played for: Lincolnshire Juniors, Newark Town, Hull City, York City, Exeter City

IN THE inflated transfer market of the modern game it would be extremely difficult to put a valuation on Freddie Speed.

Although born in the north-east, Freddie Speed's father moved down to Lincolnshire in search of work when he was a child. The youngster began to show his footballing prowess before making the short journey from Newark Town to Mansfield Town, via a circuitous route.

A play-anywhere, two-footed, dedicated professional, an opportunity arose for him to play league football with Hull City. Naturally left-footed, but capable of playing almost anywhere, Fred helped the Tigers win promotion to Division Two in 1933. He then moved on to York City, before returning to Nottinghamshire, with Mansfield Town, in time for the start of the 1936–37 season.

Slotting into the middle of the Town defence Freddie's debut season for the club coincided with Ted Harston's extraordinary goal-scoring feats at the other end of the pitch. Harston joined the immortals with 55 league goals that season – Freddie got one, at home to Southport, but would have enjoyed the sensation just as much as the great striker would ever have done. The following season, with Harston now at Liverpool, Fred got himself on the scoresheet another five times including a penalty kick winner at Southend.

In terms of statistics, that 1937–38 season saw the Stags pull in a crowd of 15,890 to watch a third round FA Cup tie, at home to Leicester City. The paying receipts were a then record amount of £1,220!

A year on, with Freddie very much part of the nucleus of the side, came another FA Cup oddity. How Stags supporters of the present era would love to see their side run out at Old Trafford! After away and home draws respectively, and a goalless second replay on neutral territory at Doncaster, Mansfield Town and Halifax Town had to meet for a second round third replay at Manchester United's ground. The match, on 21 December 1938, attracted just 1,219 fans – and the Stags lost.

The outbreak of war curtailed Freddie's career but not before he had completed a century of league appearances for Town. A great distributor of the ball and a tenacious tackler, Fred Speed was the first Mansfield Town player to be dubbed 'Mr Versatile'.

Chris Staniforth

Date of birth: 16 September 1897, Carrington, Nottingham
Died: 24 December 1954

Mansfield Town record:

Appearances: 160
Goals: 152
Debut: 27 August 1921 v Worksop Town (h) won 2–0

Also played for: Notts County, Cresswell Athletic, Chesterfield Municipal, Oldham Athletic, Shirebrook, Grantham, Sutton Town, Worksop Town, Cresswell Colliery

MANSFIELD Town's leading goalscorer of all time is Chris Staniforth. Chris liked to change clubs fairly often – he signed for Mansfield Town on no fewer than five separate occasions. One wonders just how many goals he would have scored for the club had he not moved so many times during his career!

Wherever he went, though, he scored goals, and his output for the Stags was 152 goals in only 160 games. His overall career strike-rate is equally impressive: 320 games and 226 goals!

He was an outstanding talent in schoolboy football in the Nottingham area and played a few games for Notts County as a youngster. He then moved to the Cresswell area, where he was spotted and taken on by Chesterfield.

At the age of 23 he made his first appearance for Mansfield Town but only stayed for just over a year. During the 1921–22 season he was the club's top scorer, with 25 goals from 41 Midlands League appearances.

In between moves to Oldham and Notts County, he continued to bang goals in for the Stags, helping the side to a succession of local titles and cup wins. In the days before media coverage, the most frequently asked question about a Mansfield game was, 'And how many did Staniforth score?'

Instantly recognisable by his prematurely receding hairline, Chris became club skipper and led the side on their famous FA Cup run of 1928–29. Sadly, for one so reliable in front of goal, he missed a penalty in the famous fourth round tie at Highbury against Arsenal – a penalty he shouldn't have taken. Regular club penalty taker Charles 'Pop' Anthony refused to shoulder the responsibility. Chris, as captain, asked several other players before taking the kick himself. The records tell us that his shot was hard and low but was parried and caught by Lewis in the Gunners' goal.

That rare miss shouldn't detract from Chris Staniforth's wonderful achievements in a Mansfield jersey. His final spell with the club coincided with their introduction into the Football League and he played a major role in that achievement.

In 1932 Staniforth moved to Sutton Town, and then to Worksop Town, before returning to be player-manager of Creswell Colliery. He died in 1954, aged 57.

Phil Stant

Date of birth: 13 October 1962

Mansfield Town record:

Appearances: League 61, FA Cup 2, League Cup 5, Others 2
Goals: League 33, FA Cup 0, League Cup 2, Others 0
Debut: 17 August 1991 v Scarborough (a) drew 0–0

Also played for: Reading, Hereford United, Notts County, Blackpool, Lincoln City, Huddersfield Town, Fulham, Cardiff City, Bury, Northampton Town, Brighton and Hove Albion

Managed: Lincoln City

THERE can be few players who can lay claim to receiving a standing ovation from opposing fans after scoring four goals against them, but that is exactly what happened to Phil Stant on his return to Field Mill with promotion-hunting Bury in 1995–96. It says much about the Stags fans – but it also speaks volumes for the man himself.

Phil was signed by George Foster, for what worked out to be a bargain £50,000 from Fulham. A former soldier, he came armed with grit, determination and more importantly, goals. There are few players in the history of Mansfield Town who have had an impact like that which Stant had during his time at Field Mill. He was the definitive 'terrace hero', a player idolised by supporters and a nightmare for opposition defences.

He joined in the summer of 1991 and in his first season was the spearhead behind the Stags' successful promotion campaign. His determination to succeed, coupled with his seemingly natural ability to find the back of the net, delighted the fans and brought a true winning mentality to the club.

A record-breaking seven successive away wins were achieved that season. One of them was a 4–1 thumping of Scunthorpe United. The overriding memory of that day is witnessing Phil Stant in goal celebration. His triumphal clenched-fist celebrations are now part of Mansfield Town folklore.

'Stanty' ended the season with 26 goals, a total that would have been even higher as four were taken away from him, two due to the sad demise of Aldershot and two due to the abandonment of the Autoglass Trophy game against Peterborough United.

Out of his 26 goals, he scored one hat-trick, which came against Halifax Town. Field Mill rejoiced as their hero finally got what he had been promising all season, an elusive match ball.

The Stags' quest for promotion was to go down to the final day of the 1991–92 season, but the fans needn't have worried – Stant delivered, as he scored one of the goals in Mansfield's 2–1 victory over Rochdale to clinch promotion.

Quite rightly, the hit-man gained recognition from his fellow professionals, by being voted into the PFA Divisional team of the season. How sad it was then, that in November of the following season, manager George Foster was forced to sell Stant in an attempt to ease the club's financial worries.

Stant moved to Cardiff City, one of a dozen league clubs he played for throughout a highly successful career. He did spend one other brief loan spell back at Mansfield and later went into management with Lincoln City, ending the 2003–04 season at non-league Ilkeston Town.

Freddie Steele

Date of birth: 6 May 1916, Hanley, Stoke-on-Trent
Died: 23 April 1976, Stoke-on-Trent

Mansfield Town record:

Appearances: League 53, FA Cup 9
Goals: League 39, FA Cup 5
Debut: 20 August 1949 v Southport (a) drew 1–1
Manager: 1949–1951

Also played for: Stoke City, Port Vale, England (six caps)

Also managed: Port Vale

AS A former centre forward with both Stoke City and England, it was quite a coup when Mansfield Town appointed Freddie Steele as their player-manager in time for the start of the 1949–50 season. During his heyday he had been rated one of the best strikers in the land. Indeed, the great Stanley Matthews himself rated him as the finest. The record books today still show Steele as being Stoke's greatest ever goalscorer.

He had joined the ground staff of the Potters at just 15 years of age but, after 18 years there, Freddie had been prepared to accept his first steps into management with Third Division Mansfield.

Stoke were compensated to the tune of £750 and Freddie was given the use of a club house, at 171 Sheepbridge Lane, originally bought to be used by Roy Goodall, the previous manager. Freddie's start at Field Mill couldn't have gone much better. The side won six and drew four of his first 10 games in charge, with the new boss scoring seven goals himself, in his customary number nine jersey.

After such a bright start it was a disappointment when the team began to lose a few games and slip down the table, but interest within the town was high. Over 19,000 packed into Field Mill for the visit of league leaders Doncaster Rovers. Steele had certainly raised the club's profile.

Although in the twilight of his own playing career, Freddie was still a handful for opposition defences, particularly in the air. Although not a tall man, he had an uncanny ability to time his leaps to perfection and his heading ability brought him the majority of his goals. He hit one hat-trick during his spell with Town, which came at home, against Hartlepools United.

Stags finished eighth in the table in Steele's first year in charge but performances had been encouraging. The following season things went even better. A runners-up spot in the league was a best-ever finish for the club up to that point, and they also advanced to the fifth round of the FA Cup.

Just a couple of days before Christmas in 1951 Steele stunned everyone at Field Mill when he announced that he wished to accept an offer to join Port Vale as their manager. As Mansfield still held his playing contract, a transfer fee had to be agreed upon. Eventually the price was settled at £1,599 – because Port Vale refused to meet the asking price of £1,600.

Nicknamed 'Nobby', Freddie Steele clocked up 39 goals in 53 league matches for Mansfield – not bad for someone in their mid-30s. Steele achieved further success at Vale Park, taking the side to the semi-finals of the FA Cup and lifting the Third Division North Championship.

He later quit the game to become a publican before accepting an offer to manage Vale again. After retiring from the game for the second time he moved to live in South Africa but returned to England and died in 1976.

Mike Stringfellow

Date of birth: 27 January 1943, Nuncargate, Notts

Mansfield Town record:

Appearances: League 57, FA Cup 4, League Cup 4
Goals: League 10, FA Cup 1, League Cup 1
Debut: 30 August 1960 v Rochdale (a) won 2–1

Also played for: Leicester City, Nuneaton Borough

MIKE Stringfellow is another who profited from Raich Carter's managerial philosophy of 'If they're good enough, they're old enough'. Pitched alongside Ken Wagstaff for a 'sink or swim' debut at the tender age of 17, Mike went on to enjoy a highly successful professional career and maintained his link with the Stags when nephew Ian played for the club in the late 1980s.

As Stringfellow was an outstanding schoolboy player, it wasn't really a gamble for Carter to blood the youngster so early. In fact he adapted to first-team football quicker than anyone could have hoped and was soon on his way to the First Division.

A tall, gangly left winger, Mike only played 65 times in all for the Stags, scoring a dozen goals. The scouts were hovering, however, and Leicester City nipped in with a £25,000 bid even before he'd celebrated his 19th birthday – a record fee for someone of his age.

Despite the brevity of his time in the Stags' first team, Mike did play in two League Cup matches of historical importance to the club. His future employers no doubt took a few notes when Mansfield visited Filbert Street to play their first ever tie in the new competition in October 1960. The First Division side won by four goals to nil.

The following season over 17,000 watched at Field Mill as the Stags played their first home game under floodlights. Former England skipper Billy Wright conducted the opening ceremony, then watched as Stringfellow's goal earned his side a 1–1 draw with Cardiff City and a replay at Ninian Park.

Following his transfer, Mike enjoyed great success at Leicester City, playing in the 1963 FA Cup Final against Manchester United and in two League Cup Finals. In all he appeared in 315 league games for City, scoring 82 goals. Arthur Chandler is the only other player to appear in the top 10 lists for Leicester appearances and goals.

Many feel that Mike was never the same player after he suffered a serious cartilage injury in 1968, but he continued to play for another seven years, bowing out in a match against Derby County in 1975.

He had remained with the Foxes for 14 years and, upon retiring from the game, he became a newsagent, firstly in Sutton-in-Ashfield and then in Alfreton.

Dave Syrett

Date of birth: 20 January 1956, Salisbury, Wiltshire

Mansfield Town record:

Appearances: League 65, FA Cup 3, League Cup 4
Goals: League 20, FA Cup 0, League Cup 0
Debut: 13 August 1977 v Lincoln City (h) lost 0–1

Also played for: Swindon Town, Wolves, Walsall, Peterborough United, Northampton Town

FOR AS long as English football has existed there has been a huge gulf between Mansfield Town and Tottenham Hotspur. But in season 1977–78 everything changed. The pair met on an equal footing in the Football League standings. North London's aristocrats were experiencing a lone season out of the top flight and the supposed 'colliery commoners' were enjoying the lofty heights of Division Two.

It wasn't meant to be like that – and it hasn't happened since – but when the sides clashed at Field Mill on 25 March 1978 the Stags found a hero in Dave Syrett. The match ended all square at 3–3, but Syrett's hat-trick is still adjudged to have been among the most dramatic ever scored by a Mansfield Town player. It is certainly the only one ever scored by a Stag in the second tier of our domestic game.

More recent generations have had cause to be grateful for the presence of the ITV cameras at Field Mill that day – occasionally the goals get a well-deserved airing. That afternoon was certainly Dave's finest in a Mansfield shirt, although he enjoyed a consistent season, top scoring for the club with 16 goals in the league.

Dave Syrett had begun his career as an apprentice at Swindon Town, and made several appearances for the England youth team. Two connections with the Stags are worth noting from Dave's days at the County Ground. He played under Danny Williams, a former Mansfield manager – and his form in the first team persuaded his club that they could allow Ray Clarke to move to Field Mill.

During his time at Swindon, Syrett notched 37 goals in 120 appearances. After a short and not particularly fruitful loan spell at Wolves, Dave signed for the Stags. Player-boss Peter Morris had targeted the front-man as being an ideal foil for Ernie Moss.

An injury to 'Big Ernie' meant that the partnership wasn't allowed to flourish. Dave, though, led the line well and scored 16 goals – the most by a Stag that season. He moved to Walsall midway through the next season as part of the deal which brought Terry Austin to Field Mill and later had spells at Peterborough United and Northampton Town.

Dave's playing days were ended by a back injury, sustained while playing for non-league Brackley. Settling back home in Wiltshire, he'll still get a warm glow recalling the day he bagged three against Tottenham.

Colin Toon

Date of birth: 26 April 1940, New Houghton, Derbyshire

Mansfield Town record:

Appearances: League 213, FA Cup 12, League Cup 6
Goals: League 1
Debut: 25 January 1958 v Accrington Stanley (h) lost 0–2

Also played for: New Houghton

FULL-BACK Colin Toon played for Mansfield Town for nine seasons and under four different managers. He came from a mining family and first signed for the Stags as an amateur in 1956, when he was just 16, becoming a pro the following year. Town's scouts had reacted quickly after being alerted to the news that New Houghton had a promising young right winger within their ranks.

Ironically it was felt that Colin would have more of a future as a defender and he went on to play over 200 times for Mansfield at full-back. He was thrust into the first-team spotlight at just 17 and enjoyed a brief run of seven consecutive games. The following campaign he had to bide his time, with manager Sam Weaver opting for the more experienced John Thomas. Nevertheless, Colin still made 17 league appearances, enhancing his reputation at every opportunity. Raich Carter's arrival as manager coincided with Colin's promotion to first-team regular.

Although the side were heavily beaten on the evening, Colin was a member of the line-up that participated in the Stags' first-ever League Cup fixture, away at Leicester City, in October 1960.

In terms of league position those were grim days for followers of Mansfield Town, with the side languishing near to the bottom of the Football League. However, at least there was some consistency at right-back, with Colin Toon enjoying an unbroken run of 111 consecutive league appearances, stretching between September 1960 and March 1963. One of those matches, against the soon-to-fold Accrington Stanley, was later expunged from the records.

Despite spending his formative years playing in a more advanced role on the right, Colin seldom neglected his defensive duties. Consequently, he rarely found himself in goalscoring situations. He did eventually break his goal drought in the 1962–63 season, with his only goal for the club in a 2–3 defeat away at Workington.

That campaign ended in promotion for the only time in Colin's career, but early in the new season he broke a leg at home to Brentford. Almost a calendar year later, he returned to the side at left-back, and was to play a further 26 games for the club.

One of a long line of dedicated and hard-working full-backs that have graced Field Mill, Colin remained in the Mansfield area after ending his playing days and joined a local supermarket chain. For many years he could be seen still turning out for an ex-professionals XI, helping to raise funds for charity.

Ken Wagstaff

Date of birth: 24 November 1942, Langwith, Nottinghamshire

Mansfield Town record:

Appearances: League 181, FA Cup 8, League Cup 7
Goals: League 93, FA Cup 7, League Cup 5
Debut: 30 August 1960 v Rochdale (a) won 2–1

Also played for: Hull City

QUITE simply, Ken Wagstaff was all about goals. He was a true goalscoring machine, who topped the Stags' scoring charts in successive seasons. Blooded by boss Raich Carter, at the tender age of 17, along with another talented youngster, Mike Stringfellow, Ken proved to be an instant success.

If anyone wondered whether he was capable of making the step up from the Mansfield Youth League, where he scored goals for fun for Langwith Woodland Imps, 'Waggy' soon dispelled their fears. He scored both goals away against Rochdale on his debut, and marked his first appearance at Field Mill with the winning goal against Peterborough United, 11 days later. These were the first three of 105 goals he was to score for Mansfield Town, 93 in the league.

Ken's most successful season came in 1962–63, with a display that would attract scouts from all over the world nowadays. He scored a total of 41 goals in 49 league and cup games.

Ken became the first Stag since Ted Harston 26 years earlier to score four hat-tricks in a season. His record-breaking run began away against Exeter City. In the FA Cup he scored three at Field Mill against Crystal Palace and then he put three past Oldham Athletic and four past Southport in a 6–1 victory.

Short and stocky, he was a predator. His best work came in and around the penalty box, where he was the consummate converter of the half-chance. Knock-downs, cut-backs, deflections – if they fell to Waggy the odds would be on him scoring.

As his strike partnership with Roy Chapman flourished, so did the goals. He was an ever-present in 1963–64 – bad news for defenders – and helped himself to another 29 gloriously opportunistic strikes. Inevitably the offers began to pour in and there was a great deal of sadness when Ken was allowed to sign for Hull City in November 1964.

There was some consolation in that he continued to score – and score – and score! He hit 173 goals in 378 games for the Tigers, prompting general astonishment that he didn't go on to play for one of the really big clubs or gain international recognition, although he was taken on one FA Representative tour of Australia in 1971.

As much a hero on Humberside as he was at Mansfield, Ken settled in Hull after his retirement and became a publican.

Clive Walker

Date of birth: 24 October 1945, Watford

Mansfield Town record:

Appearances: League 229, FA Cup 17, League Cup 13
Goals: League 8, FA Cup 1, League Cup 1
Debut: 9 August 1969 v Gillingham (h) won 1–0

Also played for: Leicester City, Northampton Town, Chelmsford City, Gravesend

Manager/First team coach: Northampton Town, Kettering, Dagenham and Redbridge, Maidstone
United, Dover Athletic, Chatham Town

CLIVE Walker was much more than just an accomplished defender. He was tactically sound, utterly reliable and a model of consistency – all qualities that endeared him to the fans, as well as his own teammates.

Stags manager Tom Eggleston used to lay claim to having a 'little black book', his own pocket guide to some of the players he had noted on his travels up and down the country. 'Walker', he would say, 'was in my book!'

Clive's family had moved to Leicester when he was a child and he gained international recognition for the English Schools side before joining the Filbert Street club as an apprentice, aged just 16. Fleet of foot, he loved to get forward at every opportunity. Attacking full-backs, keen to go on the overlap and whip in dangerous crosses, weren't quite as common in those days.

After three years with Leicester City, during which time he made 17 first-team appearances, Clive was allowed to seek regular first-team football and was transferred to Northampton Town. That was in October 1966 and in the following two seasons he was a permanent fixture in the Cobblers' line-up, and it was a little surprising when he was given a free transfer at the end of that second season. But out came that 'little black book' and although Walker and his family were away on holiday, a note from manager Eggleston lay on the doormat when he returned.

'We'd been away to Skegness for a couple of days', recalls Clive. 'I must admit it was a pleasant surprise to return and find myself becoming a Mansfield Town player and I didn't regret it for a moment. At that time the club were establishing themselves as something of a cup team and we had some great days, playing at Leeds United and Liverpool, in my time there.'

Clive's full-back partnership with Sandy Pate is still regarded as being among the finest ever enjoyed by the Stags. For five seasons, Walker was a virtual ever-present, missing games only rarely through injury. It was a knock, though, sustained at Cambridge United on 24 September 1974, that presented Barry Foster with an opportunity to stake a claim for a first-team place. The youngster took full advantage of the opportunity to make the left-back spot his own property.

Walker's next club was Chelmsford City, but it was not long before he was back with Northampton Town, first as coach, then for a spell as manager, before reverting to coach again.

Over the past two decades Clive has gained respect for being among the top coaches in our non-league pyramid. He concluded the 2003–2004 season as manager of Chatham Town, in the Dr Marten's League Eastern Division. During the close season he coaches American teenagers at a friend's soccer academy in Virginia.

Phil Waller

Date of birth: 12 April 1943, Leeds

Mansfield Town record:

Appearances: League 159, FA Cup 19, League Cup 9
Goals: League 1, FA Cup 1, League Cup 1
Debut: 16 March 1968 v Brighton and Hove Albion (a) lost 0–3

Also played for: Derby County, Ilkeston Town, Boston, Matlock Town, Burton Albion, Belper Town, Kimberley Town

PHIL Waller was another vital member of the Stags' giant-killing side of the late sixties. Tagged as an old fashioned wing-half, his position has a different title today. He explains 'Really I was the left-sided central defender. For much of my time with Mansfield I played alongside Stuart Boam – he really was an exceptional player. I wasn't surprised at all that he went on to have such a good career.'

Although born in Leeds, Phil's professional career began with Derby County, whom he joined as a junior in 1961. He remained at the Baseball Ground until 1968, topping the century mark in appearances and playing in a league cup semi-final for the Rams against Leeds United.

He was still highly respected within the game, so it was a significant signing when he moved to Mansfield Town for £6,000 in March 1968. They weren't great times for the club. Despite Phil's presence for the final 13 games of the season, the Stags finished 21st in Division Three, but were reprieved when Peterborough United were relegated instead, for making illegal payments. 'I remember the feeling of despondency, with us going off the field on the last day of the season, believing we were down' says Phil. 'It was only later when the Peterborough situation handed us a lifeline.'

Never a prolific goalscorer, Phil scored the first of his three goals for the club at home to Walsall, in April 1969. That match followed a couple of months after the 'West Ham giant-killing'. Most eyes had been turned towards Bobby Moore, the captain of England, at the start of the evening. By the end, after a stunning display, it was the man in the home number six jersey who was taking the plaudits, along with his weary but jubilant teammates.

Memory tells us that the Stags cruised past the Hammers that evening. Old match reports tell us that Phil did well to head away a goal-bound drive from Jimmy Lindsay, with the scores still level. 'They had a few chances early on', he remembers. 'But after that we fully deserved our win.'

In all, Phil spent four and a half seasons at Field Mill and made more than 150 appearances for the senior team. A year after the West Ham match, Phil was also in the side for another epic FA Cup day out – this time ending in defeat at Leeds United.

He left Field Mill to accept an offer of becoming player/manager at Ilkeston Town. He subsequently did the round of local non-league clubs before retiring from the game to become a partner in a prosperous motor dealership at Mickleover near Derby.

'I've always thought of myself as being very fortunate', he admits. 'I had an enjoyable career as a professional sportsman and have made a few bob from my business life.' Phil also worked as a general sales manager for Ansells Brewery, in the Potteries, but is now back among the motors, working for Beechdale Subaru in Derby.

Stuart Watkiss

Date of birth: 8 May 1966, Wolverhampton

Mansfield Town record:

Appearances: League 41, FA Cup 1, League Cup 3
Goals: League 1
Debut: 17 August 1996 v Exeter City (h) lost 0–1
Manager: January 2002–December 2002

Also played for: Wolves, Crewe Alexandra, Walsall, Hereford United

YOU won't find anyone at Field Mill with a bad word to say about Stuart Watkiss. One of the most likeable characters to be associated with the club, he served as player, youth coach and first-team manager, all in the space of six years.

Andy King did the Stags a great favour when he snapped up Stuart on a free transfer from Hereford United in 1996. A commanding central defender, Stuart had made two appearances for Wolves, his home-town club, and just three at Crewe, before establishing himself at both Walsall and Hereford United.

Shortly after his move to Mansfield, King parted company with the club and Steve Parkin took over as manager. Immediately Watkiss was installed as captain. With typical footballer's originality Stuart was tagged 'Skip', a nickname that remained with him throughout his time at the club.

Stuart's commitment and will to win made him a firm fans' favourite. Although a constant threat at dead-ball situations, he only registered one goal for Town, that coming in an away win at Darlington in October 1996.

During another away game, at Notts County in September 1997, Stuart sustained an injury to his ankle ligaments. After a 10-month lay off, his attempted comeback ended in defeat and he was forced to retire.

The club responded to this set-back by cashing in on Stuart's popularity and extensive experience by giving him the chance to coach the youngsters at Field Mill, bringing along the likes of Liam Lawrence, Craig Disley and Lee Williamson. Promotion to assistant manager soon followed and when Billy Dearden moved on to pastures new, Stuart was handed the senior side's reins.

One of the lasting memories supporters will have of Stuart Watkiss is the look of pure delight upon his face when he was carried from the pitch after the Stags had beaten Carlisle United to win promotion at the end of the 2001–02 season. True, much of the work in the first part of the season had been down to Dearden, but Stuart, aided and abetted by some of the youngsters he'd helped develop, completed the task. Credit deservedly belonged to both men.

Life was a little tougher the following season but the fans stuck by Stuart and the team, and the decision to replace him in December 2002 was deemed a little harsh by many. Typically, Watkiss accepted his fate with good grace.

Throughout his period at the club Stuart was never less than 100 percent committed to the future of Mansfield Town. For that, he will always have the respect and good wishes of all Stags supporters.

Neil Whatmore

Date of birth: 17 May 1955, Ellesmere Port, Cheshire

Mansfield Town record:

Appearances: League 76, FA Cup 4, League Cup 4, Others 15
Goals: League 20, FA Cup 0, League Cup 0, Others 1
Debut: 1 December 1984 v Blackpool (a) lost 0–1

Also played for: Bolton Wanderers, Birmingham City, Oxford United, Burnley

EIGHTEEN months into the job at Field Mill, manager Ian Greaves knew where to go shopping when he needed a striker. Neil Whatmore had starred in Greaves's Bolton Wanderers side that had won the Second Division championship of 1977–78.

A proven goalscorer, Whatmore had made more than 300 appearances for the Trotters and was considered nothing short of an icon in that part of Lancashire. Nevertheless, he'd moved on, via Birmingham City and Oxford United, to Burnley, where his opportunities were becoming increasingly limited. The time was right for Greaves to make his move.

Whatmore made his debut in a 1–0 defeat away at Blackpool in December 1984. It was not the most auspicious start to a Stags career – and it has to be said that Neil didn't score the amount of goals in a Mansfield shirt that the fans had hoped when he was signed.

He did, though, bring experience and commitment. He was the perfect foil for the tireless Keith Cassells in the promotion-winning campaign of 1985–86. Sometimes big-name strikers filter down the leagues and offer their new employers very little – but Neil was different. He appreciated that his career was coming to an end and looked to savour every last moment. His enthusiasm couldn't be faulted and rubbed off on the younger players.

Neil didn't exactly meet the criteria for a stereotypical striker. He wasn't particularly tall or overly quick – but he did have a footballer's brain and years of know-how to call upon. Like all of the best strikers, he possessed an inbred instinct to be in the right place at the right time.

Fittingly, he joined Stags at a time when he could enjoy some fleeting success. The promotion campaign was an enjoyable aperitif, while the Wembley experience was a regal banquet.

Neil had scored a winning goal in an earlier round, against York City, on the way to the Freight Rover Final. On the big day he was magnificent – covering every blade of grass before being substituted by Ian Stringfellow. Deservedly, he collected his winners' medal and entered the annals of Mansfield Town history.

He spent the 1987–88 season as the Stags' reserve-team coach, before entering the non-league game. After a successful coaching spell in South Africa he settled in the Mansfield area, coaching a number of local sides, including Forest Town Rangers, Eastwood Town and Rainworth Miners Welfare.

Steve Whitehall

Date of birth: 8 December 1966, Bromborough

Mansfield Town record:

Appearances: League 43, FA Cup 2, League Cup 2, Others 2
Goals: League 24, FA Cup 1, League Cup 0, Others 1
Debut: 9 August 1997 v Hull City (h) won 2–0

Also played for: Rochdale, Oldham Athletic, Chester City

DESPITE spending just one season on the staff at Field Mill, Steve Whitehall earned himself a place among the club's legends. Having been something of a cult hero at Rochdale, where he'd been scoring regularly for six seasons, Steve felt the weight of expectancy on his shoulders when he arrived at Mansfield – and he didn't disappoint.

With the side resplendent in their new centenary strip for the first time, Steve broke his Mansfield duck with a thunderous drive to set up a 2–0 win at Lincoln City. Although the Stags struggled to make any real impact in the first half of the season, Whitehall was scoring goals consistently and, as the season progressed, looked to be making a serious bid for a place in the play-offs.

Unfortunately, that didn't materialise – not for the want of trying, as far as the club's number 10 was concerned. If the team's overall position proved to be a disappointment, the impact Steve Whitehall had at Field Mill certainly wasn't. He made a clean sweep of all the Player of the Year awards for the 1997–98 season and his 26 goals made him an instant hero with the supporters.

There is no doubt that goalscorers become crowd favourites, but every now and then there emerges one particular scorer of goals that ignites excitement each time he touches the ball. Whitehall was such a player.

How shattering it was to see him leave the club after one season. Wage disputes didn't help and, coupled with the strain of trying to commute from his home in Warrington, when Oldham Athletic came in for him he was all too ready to make the change.

He eventually left the Boundary Park club and joined Chester City before dropping into non-league obscurity, but although he only played one season in Mansfield Town colours, he was a player who made a long-lasting impression on the Field Mill faithful.

Steve Whitehall was 30 years of age when he joined the Stags and one can't help but imagine how the relationship might have developed had he arrived a few years earlier. With Whitehall it really was a case of 'if only'.

Steve Whitworth

Date of birth: 20 March 1952, Coalville, Leicestershire

Mansfield Town record:

Appearances: League 80, FA Cup 4, League Cup 4, Others 6
Goals: League 2
Debut: 27 August 1983 v Bristol City (a) lost 0–4

Also played for: Leicester City, Sunderland, Bolton Wanderers, England (7 caps)

STEVE Whitworth arrived at Mansfield Town as part of the Ian Greaves revolution. Having had a distinguished career of over 15 years in the game with seven full England international caps, he had achieved almost everything in the game, with one notable exception – he had never scored a goal!

Playing out his entire career in the right-back position, he must have thought his chance of goalscoring glory had passed him by when he moved to Mansfield Town towards the end of his league career. But how little he knew. Although the two goals Steve scored for Mansfield Town both came from the penalty spot, fans still recall the look of sheer delight, mixed with relief, upon his face. Ironically both goals came at Field Mill, within a fortnight of each other. His first came against Hereford United in a 1–1 draw and the other was in a 2–2 draw with Exeter City.

At the time of his arrival at Field Mill, Mansfield Town was seemingly at an all-time low. Ian Greaves looked anything but the managerial magician he eventually turned out to be and the Stags, pre-season promotion favourites, were losing week in week out and playing in front of all time record low attendances.

Yet in Steve Whitworth the fans found themselves with someone they could rely on. The very fact that he'd worn the Three Lions on his shirt, and played at the highest level, gave them a boost – Steve was a Stag so everything would be all right.

In all, Steve made over 650 Football League appearances. A native of Leicestershire, he'd spent a decade with the Foxes, winning the Division Two Championship in 1970–71 and the Charity Shield the following year. His England debut came at Wembley, against World Champions West Germany in 1975.

Six more caps followed over the next couple of seasons, although the emergence of Liverpool's Phil Neal probably denied him the opportunity to make a bigger impression. Steve joined Sunderland in 1979, for £125,000, playing his part in a successful promotion campaign before joining Bolton in 1981.

For all his years in the game, his dream of finding the net failed to materialise – until he joined the Stags. His final match for Town came in May 1985, whereupon he retired from the game and moved into business.

Steve Wilkinson

Date of birth: 1 September 1968, Lincoln

Mansfield Town record:

Appearances: League 232, FA Cup 11, League Cup 14, Others 17
Goals: League 83, FA Cup 2, League Cup 4, Others 2
Debut: 3 October 1989 v Luton Town (a) lost 2–7

Also played for: Leicester City, Rochdale, Crewe Alexandra, Preston North End

STEVE Wilkinson can claim to be the first Stag in 53 years to score five goals in a Football League match. His extraordinary feat came at Field Mill on a Tuesday evening, 3 April 1990, against Birmingham City. The striker's achievement, in the 5–2 win, matched that of Ted Harston in the 1930s and left 'Wilko' a little bewildered by it all.

'It certainly took a while to sink in', he said later. 'The whole of the next day was a bit of a blur, even when I had to go down to the ground to talk to the press. I reported back for training on the Thursday and the players were still coming up to me and patting me on the back.' But as is so typical in football, it was a case of 'after the Lord Mayor's Show' in the next game. 'The following Saturday I had an awful game. It was as if I'd used up all my good luck in one game!'

With almost a century of goals for Mansfield Town, there is little doubt that Steve Wilkinson was worth every penny of his club record transfer fee of £80,000. He top-scored in five out of six seasons at Field Mill.

Signed from Leicester City by George Foster, Steve made a scoring debut during another goal-fest, the 7–2 League Cup defeat away at Luton Town in October 1989.

Steve scored 30 goals in his first season and a half with Town but it still couldn't prevent relegation at the end of the 1990–91 campaign. The strike partnership of Steve with Phil Stant enabled the club to return immediately, even though a shoulder injury deprived Wilko from playing in the final run-in.

With the Stags yo-yoing between the bottom two leagues, another drop was inevitable. Plying his trade in a side that struggled all season to find the back of the net, Steve's 11 goals weren't enough to prevent another swift return to the basement.

Season 1994–95 proved to be one of the best of his career. He cracked home 26 goals to power the Stags into the play-offs. Along the way he'd enhanced his popularity with a home hat-trick over local rivals Chesterfield. Fate matched the two same sides together in the end-of-season battle for promotion, and although Steve scored one of the Mansfield goals in the second leg of their play-off semi-final, it was the Spireites who went through.

Still only 26, Steve was allowed to join Preston North End, for a bargain £100,000, whereupon he added a Third Division Championship medal to his collection. After bowing out of league football Steve returned to Nottinghamshire, to settle, with his family, in Eastwood.

Lee Williamson

Date of birth: 7 June 1982, Derby

Mansfield Town record (to end of season 2003–04):

Appearances: League 139, FA Cup 9, League Cup 3, Others 5
Goals: League 3
Debut: 24 September 1999 v Shrewsbury Town (h) won 4–0

SCHOOLBOYS are always told to persevere. It's drilled into them from an early age that to succeed they should show their determination and follow their dreams. Lee Williamson always wanted to become a professional footballer and Mansfield Town have reaped the benefit.

Aged just 16, the world seemed a cruel place to Lee when he was released after spending three years with Stoke City's youngsters and another two at home-town club Derby County. Far from giving up on his ambitions, however, Lee made himself available for a series of trial games at Keele University.

'There were about 100 kids there', recalls Lee. 'Scouts from all over the place were invited and I was spotted by Tony Ford and Bob Shaw, who were there for Mansfield.' The good news was just beginning for the young midfielder. 'I received a letter, offering me an apprenticeship. I already knew Bobby Hassell quite well, so jumped at the chance to join Mansfield.'

In just a short time Lee experienced many of football's highs and lows, all wearing the Stags colours. 'I'll never forget actually making my first-team debut for the club, and skippering the side at just 19 was a great honour.'

On a personal level, season 2001–02 couldn't have gone much better for Lee. 'The promotion year was just amazing and I was delighted to win the Player's Player of the Year Award that season and be voted into the PFA Team of the Year.' The disappointment of relegation soon followed but, under Keith Curle in May 2004, Lee experienced the biggest occasion of his career to date.

'The play-off final at the Millennium Stadium was just the most amazing occasion I've ever been involved with. It was the biggest crowd I'd ever played in front of and the Stags fans were just great – it was buzzing!'

Naturally, the day was ruined by the result but Lee's performance was outstanding. 'Everyone was very down in the dressing room afterwards. We tried to take some satisfaction from how we'd played but the defeat was hard to accept.'

Lee is known to one and all as 'Leroy' at Field Mill and a former Stag is held responsible. 'It was Alistair Asher who began calling me Leroy, eventually everyone started to use it!'

If there's one disappointing aspect of Lee's game it's his meagre goals output. 'I don't get many', he admits. 'But they're usually worth waiting for. At Lincoln a couple of years ago I hit a screamer after playing a 1–2 with Andy White!'

Stags fans will be hoping that there are plenty more twists and turns in Leroy's Field Mill career – all of them successful ones!

Dennis Wright

Date of birth: 19 December 1919, Boythorpe, near Chesterfield
Died: August 1993, Palterton, near Bolsover, Derbyshire

Mansfield Town record:

Appearances: League 379, FA Cup 20
Debut: 12 October 1946 v Leyton Orient (a) lost 1–3

Also played for: Glentoran, Nottingham Forest

THE likes of Dennis Wright are so rarely found today. He was a truly one-club man, spending 18 years at Field Mill as a player and then a further eight as groundsman. Apart from being regarded as a terrific servant to the club, he was also an exceptionally good goalkeeper.

Dennis was denied the opportunity to make his league debut before the war, although his chance nearly came when Jack Hughes sustained a long-term injury in pre-season training, but manager Jack Poole erred on the side of caution, believing that Dennis was a little too inexperienced, so Fred Biddlestone was brought in instead.

Typical of the man, Dennis was one of the first Stags players to volunteer for the Army in October 1939, and he spent most of the war years in Northern Ireland, where he 'guested' for Glentoran, winning a Unity Cup medal in 1943. Later in the war he toured with the Army representative team and played in matches against Scotland, France, Holland and Belgium.

When on leave, he would always return to Mansfield, desperate to secure a place at Field Mill. On one occasion when the Stags were playing Leicester City at Filbert Street, and he was travelling as a reserve, Leicester were a man short, so Dennis turned out for them – at centre-forward and scored a goal!

He also turned out for Nottingham Forest during 1943–44, but peace brought Dennis the opportunity to stake a claim to be the first-choice 'keeper at Field Mill.

For the first handful of games after the war Vic Cromack played in goal but once Dennis had been handed his opportunity he became a permanent fixture in the side, except for injury.

Although he continued playing for another six seasons, Dennis was actually given a testimonial by the club in May 1950. Stoke City sent a strong side to Field Mill and a bumper crowd of 12,500 turned up to pay tribute to their goalie. The match finished level at 1–1.

Dennis played a total of 379 league games for the club and in another 20 FA Cup ties, leaving his tally one short of 400. For a long time this was a club record. He played his last senior game for the club when he was nearly 37.

Mansfield Roll of Honour

S.J. Abbott
Mark Allen
Paul Beastall
Jamie Ryan Bird
Martin John Bird
Ian Booth
Jonathan Brown
Jordan Brown
David Burrows
Chris Burton
Mick Carter
Martin Cass
Peter Cass
Steven Cunningham
Harry Cutts
Danielle Dennington
Sam Duckmanton
Christopher Eaton
Tom Ellis
Kevin Everett
John Marshall Fell
Yvonne Foster
Stephen Fowler
Stephen Gallagher
Mr M. Gardner
Dale A. Gould
Shane Hague
Si Hammond
Steve Hardy
Adam Harris
Geoffrey Heeley
David Herbert
Martyn Hill
R.L. Hudson

Ian Jackson
Peter Jackson
John Jordan
Steven Kempson
Shaun Knight
Henryk Kowalczuk
Dave Lamb
John Lamb
Gordon Leverton
Andrew Leverton
Philip Lloyd
Anthony Maddison
James Maddison
Garry Marsh
Neal Matthews
Sam Matthews
Malcolm McKee
Martin J. Neave
Tim Olive
Brian Payne
Dale Pegg
Nic Perrett
Colin Perry
Peter Stocks
Melvin David Piasecki
Andy Plant
Paul Ploughman
Mark Richard Porter
Christopher Andrew
    Porter
Jared Renshaw
Neil Roach
Stephen Roach
Jay Roberts

Craig D. Robertson
Craig K. Robertson
Dave Rogers
Peter Sharpe
Darren Shaw
Dr C.J.G. Shaw
Martin Shaw
David Slack
Chris Smith
Dave Smith
Ian Smith (Ilkley)
Dave Sugg
Kevin Swain
Peter Sweeting
Bill Taylor
Stan Tebbett
Allan Todd
Richard Todd
Gary Tyldsley
Phill Waddington
Rob Waite (Retford)
Mark Wakeling
Paige Wakeling
Jack Wakeling
Daniel Walker
Neil Walker
Ian Wilcox
Alan Michael Wilson
Eric Wint
Charles Lindley Wood
Charles William Wood
Darren Wood
Neil James Woolley
Peter Wright